WOW
WHAT A
RIDE!

REV. DR. OUIDA LEE

authorHOUSE

AuthorHouse™
1663 Liberty Drive
Bloomington, IN 47403
www.authorhouse.com
Phone: 833-262-8899

Published by AuthorHouse 09/30/2020

ISBN: 978-1-6655-0193-4 (sc)
ISBN: 978-1-6655-0192-7 (e)

Library of Congress Control Number: 2020918773

ACKNOWLEDGEMENTS

This journey would not have been possible without my loving parents, Jimmie and Pearlie B. Isaac who loved, supported and encouraged me to always do my very best in life. I am grateful for my late husband John Lee, Jr. who provided a stable home for us and our three children, Regina, Libbie and John Lee, III.

Mayflower High School – Mrs. Thelma Cox who taught me how to read in first grade. Mrs. Inez Cato who believed in me. Mrs. Novie Oneal who taught me to sing in church and at school. Mrs. Irene Johnson who said to me, "whatever is within you can never be taken away from you." Professor Algie Harkless who always taught and I accepted personally, "You're the cream of the crop and cream always rises to the top."

City of Dallas – M. W. Whitsitt, Levi Davis, Charles Tandy, MD, Ann Morgan, Joyce Rhyan, Rose Hodges, Richard Knight, Marsha Evans, Mrs. Mattie Nash.

Salem Institutional Baptist Church - Mrs. Estella Davis who intrigued my mind through dynamic Sunday School lessons at Salem Institutional Baptist Church. Mrs. Clearone Davis and Mrs. Margaret Walker who believed in me and said, "Weet, you can do it." Rev. Dr. Michael Wayne Walker who said, "Go to Perkins School of Theology where they will teach you how to think, and not what to think." And Ms. Louise Williams who said, "go to school" when I had no money. Dr. Hazel Partee, Mrs. Jozell Townsell, Mrs. Mary Louise Williams, Mrs. Marie McGain, and Mrs. Sarah P. Murphy. Missionary Society Mrs. Leon Kennedy, Mrs. Maple Barnes, Mrs. Ada Collins, Mrs. Mozella Evans and Mrs. Ollie Ashley. And Ms. Lucy Cain who had just graduated from Fisk University and returned home became a close friend.

St. Luke Community United Methodist Church - Rev. Dr. Zan

Wesley Holmes, whose response to my call to Ministry, "I will never question your call." Rev. Dr. Janet Bell Odom and Rev. Elzie Odom, Rev. Dr. Jacquelyn Donald Mims, Dr. Paula Dobbs Wiggins, Dr. Thomas Spann and Ms. Monya Davis Logan, the Wednesday Night Prayer and Praise Ministry, Mature Adults Ministry, United Methodist Women and the Sunday School and Women's Choir.

St. James and Haven Chapel Charge - Mrs. Cora Bell, Mrs. Pauline Neblett, Mrs. Malinda Gabriel, Mrs. Gloria Walker, Ms. Rhonda Williams, Ms. Hattie Powell, Mrs. Alpha Jordan, Wash Mckee, Ms. Phiebie Hutchins, the Simms Family all of the St. James and Haven Chapel Churches, that, allowed me to practice and learn ministry in your midst. We learned from each other and became successful in ministry in Sherman and Denison, Texas.

The Hamilton Park Church offered me many opportunities to work with a dynamic team led by Rev. Dr. Ronald Henderson. The support of Mrs. Gloria Walker as we traveled to Boston while doing research for my doctoral studies. Mrs. Nellie Thompson, my Sunday School teacher. Colonel and Mrs. James Adams without whose help I would not have completed the writing of my dissertation. Mr. & Mrs. Joseph Nash who supported me in so many ways. Mr. & Mrs. Larry Haynes who supported the vision of the Status and Role of Women. Mr. & Mrs. Eugene Vance, Mr.& Mrs. Curtis Smith, Mr. & Mrs. Reggie Hopkins, Mr. & Mrs. Cecil Mc Quilcan, Mr. & Mrs. Larry Haynes, Ms. Shirley Pleasant, Mrs. Ruth Robinson, and the women of the SROW Ministry, Ms. Lois Johnson, the Golden Girls, the Prayer Ministry, Ms. Cathy Parker, my driver, the Women's Choir and the Male Chorus. My Sunday Lunch Bunch, Charlotte Brewster, Carolyn Bryles and Ernestine Bullard. And so many that I loved and you loved me in return, especially the Little Children. Oh my what a ride!!!

St. Luke Community UMC – Rev. Dr. Tyrone D. Gordon, I am thankful that I was asked to serve on your staff. It was a blessing to take Mission trips along with the congregation to Africa, Brazil and the many places across the United States to receive specialized training for Ministry.

United Methodist Church of the Disciple - Brother Phillip Burke who had such a calming spirit during turbulent times. Mr. Patrick Cohen and Dr. Shelia Brown, both who served as Chair of Staff Pastor Relations

Committee Church. Darnell Walker, Keith Sharp, Van Townsend and John Pierce who served as Finance Chairs, Sheila Hector Treasurer. The music Ministry under the direction of Bernard Brown and Regina Lee as musician. Phillip Burke and Monica Guilbeaux, who served as Church Council Chairs at Church of the Disciple. Such dedicated person with deep character, persons of great faith. Monica who along with her husband Joe raised two children who also dedicated themselves to service in the church. Deborah and Keith Sharp who served as Evangelism Team, Prayer Ministry and Community Outreach. Lisa Perkins who decorated the Sanctuary and Scott Perkins who sang in the Male Chorus. Jim and Glenda Gilbert who were such strong supporters and committed to Finance, Ushers and Choir. Evangelist Ocie Hogan, Minister of Prayer and dedicated servant, along with her husband Cornell, the drummer. Mrs. Eartha Pitts Mitchell, who came to us from Houston, TX, a dedicated member of the church who served in many ministries, but especially loved the Platinum Plus Ministry. Such a profound educator and friend who dedicatedly read my manuscript, made corrections and recommendations. But even more, I consider her a friend who cheered me on many times when I was so down and disappointed. Jan Gosha, who retired from her Federal job came and gave volunteer service to our church for over a year. She was so competent, capable and appreciated while I was running all over the North Texas Conference to meetings. Sheila Hector, a dedicated member came and gave several years as a volunteer to our church after her job moved. She was so very competent and willing to help all of the members of the church. Her cheerful disposition made a huge difference during very difficult times when I as the lone full time staff attempted to keep things moving forward. I knew God as a provider and the full revelation came to reality as these women gave of themselves unreservedly to make a difference in the life of our congregation. During my last years at the church Ms. Carla Mitchell and Mrs. Doris Burke came to offer their services to the congregation; they were tremendous help. The weekly bulletin and the prayer concerns that were distributed weekly to the congregation was completely handled by them. Lay Servants Ministry was very important to the life of our congregation. Michael Matthew was both a Lay Servant who always assisted me when we baptized in the outside pool. Other Lay Servants who assisted in the Proclamation of the word were John and Dorothy Pierce, Phillip Burke, Jim Gilbert, Deborah Sharp, Ocie Hogan, along with Youth Servants Devin and Courtney Guilbeaux, and Maya Townsend. Because of the dedication of all of these volunteers, I had the opportunity of giving myself more fully to ministry within the church and the community. Thank you

The ministry that I led was done well through committed people. I could not have done it without you. You made the ride possible. And, "Wow What A Ride.!!!"

I love poetry and it has embraced my own story. A favorite poem written by poet Langston Hughes came to my attention at about the age of 40. The poem was entitled Mother to Son, as you read through this story, you will recognize why I believe that it is indicative of my life story.

I was born in Henderson, Rusk County, Texas, often referred to as East Texas by those of us hail from the Piney Woods of East Texas. This is a large geographical area often encompassing Marshall, Longview, Henderson, Tatum, Carthage, Mount Enterprise and all of the other small towns in between. My parents were Jimmie and Pearlie B. Isaac. We grew up in the country around loving families, the Beckworths, Stroliers, Adams, Flanagan, McAlister, Jones, Johnson and Sanders Families. We were surrounded by relatives, especially my mother's siblings. The long days of the summer were spent harvesting crops, peas, corn, tomatoes. And the early springs were spent planting gardens, especially on Good Friday, with vegetables that would be harvested for meals and preparing for the winter months.

Mother loved a garden and we grew beans, greens, tomatoes, cabbage, squash and potatoes. One of my greatest joys was digging the potatoes that grew underneath the ground. There were no convenience stores or fast food restaurants, so we ate the food that the land produced. There were no fountains out of which the water flowed, but water came from springs down the hill from the house, and wells in the yard from which water was drawn, and outside facilities for toilets. Water in the house was a pail and a dipper for drinking. Later in my teen years, we got inside plumbing.

I shall always remember our first house. It was a one-room shack that stood on a foundation with steps that led into the house. I was really a tiny little girl and my legs were not long enough to scale the steps, so I crawled up the steps to get into the house. There was a potbelly stove that sat in the middle of the room with a stove pipe that extended outside through the roof for ventilation. We had no concept of economics, but there was always food on the table.

I am not certain exactly when we moved out of that house, but I do recall the years that we lived in the Jenkins house. It was a bit less remote. The house was much more spacious and my father was working for the Green Family on their farm. There was no electricity, the only light came from the windows and the open door during the day and from kerosene lights during the night. The light would sit on the mantle in the living/bedroom, over the fireplace. It was a light that moved to the kitchen when something needed to be retrieved from there, and the bedroom for us children when it was time for bed.

Throughout my life our family attended church. The Antioch Baptist Church where the Rev. Fred Brown was Pastor met the first and third Sundays of every month. My mother was a member there. And the Fredonia Baptist Church where the Rev. E. M. Hooper was the Pastor. This was my daddy's church. The family attended and participated in both churches. Daddy and Mama sang in the choirs and mother was a member of the Women's Missionary Union. We attended Sunday School at mama's church. I loved both churches but my daddy's church had the more vibrant choir. They sang in Choir Confederations. As a tiny child, I recall following my parents into the choir stand and singing with them.

Saturday nights we listened to "Hoss Allen" Gospel music on WLAC out of Nashville, TN. And Sunday mornings we would listen to the Caravans on the local radio broadcast. It was not unusual for us to listen to the Rev. C. L. Franklin preaching, "The Eagle Stirreth Her Nest", my favorite of all times. Every summer during the month of August, both churches celebrated annual homecomings with dinner served on the grounds. Our friends would come from all around to get a meal that during the 60s and 70s was served out of the trunks of cars. The dressing and the potato salads never spoiled, though it had been in the trunk since early morning until about 2 p.m. The food was warm from the summer heat and everyone feasted, floating from car to car getting a slice of chocolate, pineapple cakes or sweet potato pies.

We loved the Revivals and those were the times that we kids joined church. We were placed on the front rows until we walked up to the preacher and joined church. Afterwards, we could take the back seats in church and write notes. There were great preachers who were invited to preach, and the most famous one for the Fredonia Church was the Reverend O. L. Holliday of Houston, TX. Those were exciting times because our little boyfriends would come to our churches and we would get to sit together as teenagers.

I joined the Antioch Church with my mother and will always remember my Baptism. Thank God we had recently built a new church with a baptismal pool inside. I was thankful because a couple of years earlier, I had gone to the Baptismal Service at a creek and knew that I would never be able to get in there. It did not matter that the Pastor and the Deacon were in the creek, but I knew snakes were there too. I digress. The day I was Baptized at the age of 12 Rev. Brown and Deacon Oneal were in the pool. I was so fearful of the water. Rev. Brown placed his hand over my mouth and dunked me and I must have drawn my breath through my nose and caught a mouth full of water. I came out gaggling. I have often joked about the fact that I went in as a "dry devil" and came out a "wet devil."

My understanding has grown over the years, and I now know that Baptism is a ritual of the church. For the Baptist the rite is called Believers Baptism. As a Methodist we understand that it is one of the two Sacraments of the Church and is an act of God through the grace of Jesus Christ and the work of the Holy Spirit. It is an act that only needs to be performed once because though performed by human hands it is an act of the Holy Spirit.

One of my greatest joys in church was singing in the choir. Although my mama and daddy sang before me, I had a great desire to sing, but the songs always seemed to be pitched too high for me. I later learned that all of the music that the pianist played were in the wrong key for me. I needed the flats, but the music was in sharps and after all, the Jones girls had all of the lead parts. I was a good background supporter.

The Jenkins house was the house we lived in when I began school. We learned to read by lamp light. An amazing thing that I noticed about the lamp light was if you wanted it to brightly illumine the room, it was important to clean the globe from the inside. Rational thinking would believe that it was necessary to turn the wick up in the lamp for greater light. However, if the wick was turned too high it would smoke up the globe reducing the illumination. Great life lessons are learned through simple things. However, Jesus taught us best, "Let your light shine before others, so that they may see your good works and give glory to your Father in heaven," Matthew 5:16. This verse invites us into a humble relationship, where it is unnecessary to force ourselves into visibility. As with the lamp, we cannot force our light to shine, but hear the voice of God which share, "Humble yourselves before the Lord, and He will exalt you," James 4:10. It was in that humble abode that my mother would sit with me for hours and allow me to recite poems for oratorical competitions. Who knew that even in that time and season, God had begun to prepare me for a future that was uncertain and a journey often uncharted.

This indeed was a humble time, no electricity, ice delivered to our house by an iceman, and food delivered by a grocery man. Can you imagine that a truck would come weekly to our community for us to purchase staples, cheese, flour, cornmeal, oatmeal, dried processed sausage, bologna and canned goods? This was real country, no paved roads, but dirt roads that were graded for ease of travel.

Our next place of residence was with our paternal Great Grandmother, Mrs. Minnie "Lit" Adams fondly called "Nanny" by all of us children. My grand nanny was very loving and affectionate toward me. She had raised my daddy in her own home, and now we had come to live with her. Nanny was married to Mr. Joe Adams, a man very light in hue with long straight hair. He died shortly after we moved in. These were times of fond memories. My grand nanny was a mid-wife; she delivered babies, and animals. Nanny also loved to quilt and her quilting frame hung from the ceiling rafters of her house. She would sit for hours quilting and I would watch. The moment that she would get up, I would sit down and dabble in her quilt. I was making a mess, but it never bothers her, she allowed me to be me. I did not know it then, but in retrospect, I believe that she was being a midwife to me in a social way. Allowing me to develop into the person that God was making me. I can almost hear her words to a woman who watched as I was attempting to follow her quilting. The woman asked, "why don't you make that 'gal' quit making a mess?" Her response was, "leave her alone." As a preacher woman, I recall reading those words in Biblical Scripture. John 12:7 and Mark 14:7 records those words, "leave her alone," as spoken by Jesus in relation to the woman who broke the alabaster box and poured expensive ointment on the feet of Jesus. You may recall the story, Judas was upset because the woman whose ointment was worth a year's wages, poured it on the feet of Jesus. And Jesus response to those listening was, "leave her alone. She did this in preparation for my burial." Often the words of Jesus are misunderstood. Mary, the sister of Lazarus wanted to honor Jesus with that which she possessed. She may not have even understood what her actions represented, but she used her gift to honor Jesus.

As I have grown, I have come to understand that the words of Jesus can be understood in profound ways, especially when there are those who are against the actions that you are taking. And for many women, it has been negative words from those whom you expected to support you that have caused you to give up your dreams, your mission in life. But at the tender age of about five, those words spoken to me by my Paternal Great Grandmother have anchored my soul and given me the freedom to be. She indeed was a mid-wife, who died too soon to see the one whose life she so greatly influenced.

Some may say, you were too young to know the influence that your great-grandmother had on you. Psychologically speaking, children between the ages of 4-5 children begin to think about other thoughts and feelings and that is when the theory of mind begins to develop. (Lauren Lowry, Tuning in to Others – How Young Children Develop Theory of Mind.) The foundation of learning to be me had its impetus. That freedom allowed me to take on difficult challenges throughout my life. My great grand nanny said, "leave her alone," and I never looked back. It made no difference that we did not have electricity, or refrigeration in our home, I was free to be me and to take on the challenges of life that I chose.

Getting to school was not without its' obstacles. In order to catch the school bus, we had to walk about a half of a mile, going through a gate, crossing a creek and a cattle guard in order to get to the bus stop. Often in the spring there would be rain storms, but we still had to walk to catch the bus. On several occasions when it rained, the creek would overflow the bridge, but it was the only way to get home. My oldest brother, Elnoris would cross the creek first because he knew that when the heavy rains would come, sometimes the boards in the bridge would wash away. He was our big brother and would walk through the murky waters to see if it was safe for us to cross. Armed with a long stick, he would walk into the water, tapping all around to make sure the boards were there. Sometimes the water would be half-way his leg, and swift running, but with the stick anchoring him, he would assess for our safety. He would then come back to get us, putting my younger brother, Jimmie, on his shoulders, and advising me to hold onto his shirt tail, we would walk. If a board was missing, he would advise, "step wide," and we would safely span the divide. In retrospect, I think of him as our guardian Angel. I am reminded of the many ways that God protects us along the journey of life. The Scripture from the book of Exodus 23:20, "See, I am sending an angel ahead of you to guard you along the way and to bring you to the place I have prepared." At the time, it was big brother duties, in the rearview mirror, I see the hand of God who not only guided him, but is guiding each of us throughout life.

After crossing the bridge, there was a hill to climb that was about a 45 degree incline. And as always there is a story to be told. My parents owned an old 1946 Ford pickup and of course it was a standard shift. While they were working, my younger brother Jimmie learned how to drive it. It had to roll partially down the hill and be double clutched in order to start. And he was good at it, but when it came my turn, I was afraid of the hill and unable to get it started. Therefore, I could not drive the truck, but that never stopped me from trying. I finally learned to drive when my parents bought a car with an automatic shift. My most difficult task was holding the car in the unimproved dirt road. I was so happy to be driving, and always the talker, I talked incessantly while constantly moving the steering wheel and grinning.

Some of the parents in our community were really poor, and we were part of that group. Our summers were filled with working in the cotton fields where we earned money to purchase our school clothes. Although there was no mass growth of cotton in Henderson, we would go each year to Commerce, TX to work in the cotton fields. My dad was doing construction work, when it was not raining, but he was known as a common laborer, making limited funds. Therefore, mother and her sister Christine would take us to Commerce and live on the property of "Mr. Vick" and work his field.

On our initial visit to Commerce, I was too young to drag a sack, so for the most part, my brother Jimmie and I sat at the weigh station. The house that we lived in was made of tin and had two bedrooms that had dirt floors. The only room with a floor was the kitchen. My mother and her children were in one room and my Aunt Christine were in the other with her children. These were desperate times and our parents were trying to survive. The Vicks paid $2.00 per hundred pounds of cotton pulled. Each person kept tab on the amount of cotton picked and they would be paid on Fridays. Saturdays would be the day that we would go to "town." Greenville, TX, the city with a sign that was hung as a banner over the city, "The Blackest Land and the Whitest People." One would hardly ever forget a sign with those word printed for the world to see. Mother would put clothes on layaway for us to return to school in the Fall.

The house we lived in was at the back of the big white farm house and one particular incidence stands out in my memory. It was a particularly stormy night and Mr. Vick came to the house and invited us to join them in the storm house. It was a house that was completely unnoticeable with exception of the fact that it had a tin door laying on the ground. The tin door covered an underground shelter. It was probably 10 feet down a set of wooden stairs. There was preserved food there and the only light was a lamp. We all cramped into the house because the winds were raging and thunder and lighting was all around. We were fearful and kept quiet. I am not sure how long we stayed down under, but I was relieved to get out after the storm passed over. Psalm 91 comes to mind the words of the Psalmist, "He that dwelleth in the secret place of the most High shall abide under the shadow of the Almighty. I will say of the Lord, He is my refuge and my fortress; my God; in him will I trust." That is what the Vick Family provided for our family, a place of safety and shelter from the storm.

The Vicks were kind people and I recall that he would bring ice cold "soda water" to our family as they worked the fields. When my brother Jimmie and I grew up we were given a cotton sack and assigned to work a row. And may I share with you that the rows seemed to go on forever. My brother Jimmie and I were slow and dreaded the work, it was hot and laborious. Elnoris, on the other hand was good help and he and mother earned most of the money from our work in the cotton field. We were learning even then the importance of being good employees. The Bible teaches us, "A labourer is worthy of his hire,' Luke 10:7 (KJV). But we could hardly wait to return home where life was easier.

Throughout my high school years, I was drawn to the academics. And I always enjoyed the challenge of oratorical speaking which all began when I was in elementary school. My mother had the patience to Job to sit and listen to me repeat pages of long poems as I prepared for competition. I loved competing in the Interscholastic League, and though I never won first place, those were great experiences. "School Closing" programs also allowed us to showcase our talents and I loved have a lead role in the plays. I shall always remember the evening that I shared the poem, "The Black Man's Plea for Justice." It was on one of the evenings when the white Superintendent, Trustees and families were invited to our school to have dinner and to watch us perform a program. I stood courageously before the audience and the words reverberated over the auditorium. The words were strong and I spoke with clarity the words of the poet E. D. Tyler. I did not know it then, but through those deeply stirring words, God was preparing me to be a person who would willingly standup and speak up for Justice. And even now, as I reflect upon some of the many times that I spoke in defense of "Just," and against "Unjust" causes, I realize that you are not always the winner in the situations, but there is a feeling that one is living out one's purpose in life.

It was in this segregated school, Mayflower High School of the Tatum Independent School District, one building that housed grades one through twelve that I learned my greatest lessons. We had teachers who dedicated their lives to making a difference in ours. Not only were we taught to stand up straight and look the people with whom we were communicating in the eyes. We were infused with words that would reverberate in my life for years to come, "you're the cream of the crop, and cream always rises to the top," Professor Algie Harkless. We did not compete with other races, we were all on the same team, and therefore, we were given the opportunity to be real leaders and help to shape our own destinies. We were encouraged to believe that education was the key and that we could be whatever we wanted to be, if we were willing to work hard enough for it. May I say that some 53 years later, I can agree that with Jesus on our side, nothing is impossible.

Home Economics was one of my favorite classes and I was sure to be a high school teacher. I loved sewing and cooking, exploring new recipes and making my own clothes. I made the best caramel cream pie (wish I had the recipe now). High School was fun, filled with activities, including Marching Band, School Choir and doing special summer projects with Home Economic. Academics were the highlight of my life. I was good in Mathematics and loved Algebra. I loved learning the Social Sciences, the history of our Country and exploration of the Sciences. Though not my favorite English/Literature became an ingrained part of my studies. I tried to learn Spanish, but it failed to hold my interest and I was never any good at sports. Those were the adventurous years. We loved traveling with the football team and band that performed at the games. I was never a cheerleader, however, I cheered from the stands and loved to get the stadium engaged in cheering for our team.

I was a real 'chatty' person in High School and will always remember how several of us girls would sit in Mrs. Irene Johnson's English class and attempt to talk without moving our lips. On afternoon in her class, she called me to her desk. She said. "stand right here," and she began to pinch my inner thigh. When I started to scream out she said, "you had better not make any noise." (This would not have been allowed in our schools today and she would have been disciplined by todays' standards) But life might have been quite different for me, if I had not learned discipline. I returned to my seat and did not try that trick again.

I grew up in a home with parents who had minimal education, but who were committed to our success. They had great desires for their children to go to college. And it was my goal not to disappoint them. I worked extremely hard in school to make the top grades and succeeded in accomplishing them in most of my classes. My high school English teacher whispered in my ear, "you are supposed to be the Valedictorian of your class, but they are going to give it to another classmate."

Her words were, you cannot do anything about it, but I want you to know that they can never take anything away from what you know. I kept the secret to myself and was quite disappointed. One never knows the power of words spoken, that is until you read it in the Bible, Proverbs 18:21, "Life and death are in the power of the tongue, and those who love it will eat its fruit." I chose life from the power of those words and they have formed part of my mantra for life. I did not

May 1967 High School Graduation

tell my parents about the incident until later in life, but the power of those words set me on a quest for success in life.

My father, who earlier in life had been a common laborer in construction had become a cement finisher. He was earning higher wages and was one of the finishers who helped to build bridges along Interstate Highway 20 from the Louisiana State Line to El Paso, Texas. Mother on the other hand worked as a housekeeper for the C. E and Donnie Rogers and later for Glen Rogers (over 50 years) in order to provide for our family. Yet, their intent was to assure that their children were educated. They learned of grant funds that were available to poor children in the state of Texas. And my mother and daddy took me to Nacogdoches, Texas to Stephen F. Austin College so that we could apply for the Pell Grant, and I was an award recipient. Since I had already taken the ACT, I made application to North Texas State College. A few weeks later, I received notification from NTSC that I was accepted and told the items that I needed to bring upon my arrival.

Immediately after High School, I headed for Houston, Texas to live with my Cousin William McAlister and his wife Dollee. They welcomed me to live with them and their two boys. Each morning that first summer, we made our way to the B & B Café on Cullen Boulevard. The first stop was at the local grocery store to purchase the food that was to be prepared for lunch. The people who frequented the place were an interesting bunch. Some came for a liquid lunch. And one special customer, the barber next door would request a dipping bowl to wash his fingertips before meals. The evening customers came to drink, listen to music or play pool. I was living in the bright lights of Houston, because at the close of the evening there were still places to go and things to do and see. Some businesses stayed open until 5 a.m. and how did I know, because a few times we helped them close.

I was now living in the bright lights of Houston, Texas, I shared with my parents that I was not going to school. Where had my motivation gone? Was it really the bright lights of Houston, or had I lost my focus? As a person who had a real desire for education, it must have been a real disappointment to my parents when I did not pursue education immediately after high school.

Naiveté, a bit of foolishness and a lack of knowledge, allowed me to take a different path. I told mother that I was going to take a Nurses' Aide Training Course and she provided the funding for me to do so. Although upon graduation from the program, without practical experience, there was nothing that I could do with it. I lived a foolish, immature life. Like so many young people who are away from parents for the first time in life. I had lots of cousins in Houston and Billy owned a Café. At lunch every day we served a hotmeal, in the evenings, we sold lots of beer. There was a pool table where I attempted to gain my skills. There were many interesting characters who came through those doors and I learned a lot by watching them. People who aimlessly drifting in drink beer. Old men who would show up at the first of the month when the Social Security Check arrived with a woman in tow, only to be shoved aside when younger men arrived.

My weekly call home was to my mother to whom I would share, "Life is so hard." The dream of education had been pushed to the back of my mind. By now I had my first real boyfriend and my life took a totally different path. There were late nights home and jazz clubs on Sunday afternoon. Church rarely came to mind. I was living life, hanging in clubs dancing until it was almost daylight. Life was whimsical, far removed from the piney woods and country life of Henderson. I was living in the big city with bright lights, on my own.

It was in Houston that I met my first husband. Actually, he was my first real boyfriend. He was not very tall, about 5'6" with soft dreamy eyes. He wowed me into loving him. We were married in late 1967. Soon came the first child. She was a beautiful bright-eyed baby girl. We named her Regina and I believe that life was to be great. I wanted to raise our baby girl the way that I had been raised, in church. I found a church not far fro the apartment that we rented. I joined on Sunday and never attended again. My husband Willford Norris did not attend with me. The baby and I went alone. I cannot remember a thing that was said on that Sunday, but I knew from parents that children needed to grow up in church.

Our marriage did not really stand a chance because my husband was an only child and his mother ruled his life. We lived with her for the first few months of our marriage. And of course, he could do no wrong. Wherever we had arguments, she always took his side. I insisted that we move to our own place. I was unskilled and was not old enough to have a real job. Through a newspaper article, I found a position as a short order cook. Since this was my first job, it is almost certain that I made my share of mistakes. We were to get the food prepared and on the plate and in the window so that it could be served. I did my best, but that job did not last for long.

My first husband. Wilford Norris, whom I married at the age of 18, was a truck driver who drove a bobtailed truck and made local runs. For a while after we moved into the apartment he would come home for lunch and early after work. After a period of time he showed up at lunch, and I would not see him until the next day at lunch. Many evenings I spent looking out the window for him. I would leave the light on hoping that he would come home. Where was my husband, the father of our tiny baby girl?

After the heartbreak of a broken relationship, fights, and many disappointments, I knew it was time to go home to my parents. Whenever I spoke with his mother about our relationship she always took his side.

There had been a fight the night before the day I left. We were with another couple and when we got home, he went by his mother's and picked up a shotgun and laid it across his chest. The next morning in the behavior of an abused woman, I went to the apartment and cooked a meal. His mother came by later and said that they were going out. When they left the apartment, I borrowed a trunk from my cousin, and boxes from everyone I knew.

With two black eyes, I packed my bags, and my beautiful bright-eyed daughter and the contents of the apartment and called my cousin Billy to take me to the bus station. I purchased my ticket first and my cousin backed his long bed pickup truck into the bus loading zone. When the baggage handler saw me with the two blackened eyes, and the small baby, he stamped all 21 bags, and boxes to Henderson, inclusive of a several suitcases, (luggage that was to be packed for college). He never asked a question, it could have been that he also had a daughter, a sister, or mother who needed to escape. At the time, I had never heard the words, "Domestic Violence," but perhaps he had. Or, maybe he had a young daughter, or simply felt sorry for me. He quietly stamped everything and handed me the stubs.

It was a long ride to Henderson, with a little baby. When we arrived, I called my mother and they made several trips to get all of my things, but we were home and safe. I shall never forget because it was a Sunday afternoon, and on Monday, I began my job search. With no transportation, I borrowed the family car to go to "town," and look for a job. The only job that was available in Henderson was a dishwasher at the Donut shop. They said I would arrive at 5:30 am and would wash dishes until I finished at about 1 pm and would be paid $1 per hour. What a grave disappointment. I knew that I was better than that and could do better. The High School Valedictorian earning $1 per hour

In reflection upon that time, I now realize that my mother wanted life to be better for me than her own had been. She shared that I should go to school to be a Nurse, but I could see no possibilities for how I would accomplish that goal. My focus then changed to Dallas, where my brother lived. My sister-in-law said she could help me get a job and she knew that St. Paul Hospital was hiring. On that Sunday afternoon when I left, mother gave me $4 possibly all that she could spare and I left with my brother Elnoris and his wife Mertie.

Leaving my little girl behind with my mother and siblings, I arrived in Dallas. On Monday, we hopped the bus, with my Sister-in-Law, Mertie bound for the Hospital District and St. Paul Hospital was hiring. I began working as a Nurse's Aide a few days later. This was a new experience for me, because my training had all been in a classroom environment, now I am actually working with patients. The pay, $1.67 per hour. Having never worked in a public place, if someone made me angry, I would go home. They allowed me to do so the first two times. On the third occasion, the supervisor said, "If you go home, you will not be allowed to come back." I settled down and did my work, because I had a little daughter to care for. Even then I was learning the lessons of being responsible. I needed my job. Although my mother had my daughter, Mrs. Jessie Beckworth who agreed to keep Regina for $10 per week. Regina's formula cost $1.20 per can, and diapers and baby food to buy.

One morning as I was on my way to work, at approximately 5:30 a.m. I was standing at the bus stop on the corner of Hatcher and Imperial Streets when I was approached by a man. It was dark and I had a 7 a.m. shift at the hospital. As he walked up to me, I looked at my watch. The man asked "what time is it?" I said, "It's about 5:30 and the bus will be here at about 5:45." He had his hands in his coat and pointed as if he had a gun and said,

"Come and go with me, we are going to go down this alley and F###." I had my purse in my hands and I pleaded with him to take it. I knew that my brother lived across the street and I said, "Please take my purse." And he was walking ahead and pulling me by my coat, I jerked away from him and began to scream "Help!" "Help!" Mertie heard me and she quickly woke my brother. He yelled, "Here I come!" The man grabbed me and knocked me down in the street and attempted to drag me by my hair. I had a wig on and he pulled it off. Swiftly he hit me with his fists on both sides of my face and ran, because my brother clad in his underwear was running toward me. This situation brings to light the Scripture, Psalm 46:1 "God is our refuge and strength, a very present help in trouble."

If you are wondering has God been there for me, reflect and you will find that between each line of our lives God has provided shelter, provisions, protection, encouragement, deliverance in our lives. I am so thankful that my brother was there for me.

I was very thankful that my mother was willing to keep my daughter while I attempted to get established. Money was short with such low wages, but somehow we made it. I would take the bus home every time I had a weekend off to see my child whom they had spoiled rotten. When she came to live with me she did not want the morning dew to get on her socks and God forbid that a bit of dirt would find its way to her socks.

During the time that I was working at St. Paul, my father was killed. It was a Sunday afternoon during Memorial Day weekend of 1969. The announcement came to me from my brother in a phone call from home. This was the first major crisis of my life, with many others to follow. I was called to the front desk and the voice over the phone said, "Ouida, daddy got killed." I screamed and passed out. When I came to, I heard the nurse saying, "Who is this and what did you tell her?" Everyone came and offered me dimes and quarters to make another phone call home to find out what had happened. It was tragic, a man whom my family often visited had shot and killed my father. My brother came to pick me up, and one of the Nuns at St. Paul walked me to the door and stayed with me, and I shall never forget the words from Sister Mary Paul, "Ouida, the Lord giveth, and the Lord taketh away, blessed be the name of the Lord." That was hard for me to hear at that time, but somehow, those words brought a strange sense of comfort.

It probably had been a month earlier that I had joined church at Salem Institutional Baptist Church, where I became a member in June 1969. The people there were kind to me. I loved to sing, therefore, I joined the gospel choir. My mother had hosted the Women's Missionary Society at home a few times, so I joined the Missionary Society. I had nothing better to do, so I absorbed myself in the ministries of the church, Sunday School, Baptist Training Union, Prayer Meeting and the Missionary Department.

I made my journey home with my Brother Elnoris and his wife Mertie. It was a solemn trip, I sat in the back seat and wondered how all of this could have occurred, because only a week earlier the entire family had been together and we had such fun together. I was my daddy's oldest girl, the one he spoke to about not working as a Maid, but to work in an office. The daughter who talked a lot like my daddy. The one who could not believe that he was actually dead. The one who the morning after his death went to the funeral home to see him for myself. The one who visited him every day until his funeral. The Mortician who would allow me to go into the room and view him on the cooling board. I noticed that his mustache was growing over his top lip, he always kept it neatly trimmed along his lip line. It is amazing the things that one notices when there is no conversation. Observing the simple things in life and being curious has led me on a journey of faith. A journey where things could not be easily explained. A journey of wondering and sometimes wandering. A journey of walking in the unexpected and finding a whole new world that I was completely unaware existed. I call it a Journey of Faith.

The day after my daddy's death, the news on the radio kept reporting that my dad had been killed and no charges had been filed. I told mother that we should go and file charges. When we arrived at the jail, the Sheriff told us that the murderer was no longer in jail. He said, "Mr. Greene needed him to plow his fields." We were devastated and returned home.

The memories of the week flood my mind. His older brother Warren arrived from Belton, Texas and when he came in, I screamed and cried. I had never noticed how much they looked alike. The funeral home came and brought his shoes, a sign that dad would not be returning home. I screamed and cried. Mother held it together for all of us, until the Family car arrived to pick us up. She cried, a soft mournful cry that I will never forget. Many things must have flood her mind. She was 41 and was left with three children at home to raise alone. Her income was so limited. She lived in the country. How would she make it off the $5 per day that she was earning?

My heart hurt and leaving her on that Sunday was one of the saddest days of my life. I hurt for mother, but I could not stop the pain. The one thing that I had was my new faith. Faith in the God who had given and had taken away and "blessed be the name of the Lord." And there was a song, I believe that the words were written on his program – "I come to the garden alone, while the dew is still on the roses. And the voice I hear falling on my ear, the Son of God discloses. And he walks with me and he talks with me and he tells me I am his own. And the joy we share, as we tarry there, none other has ever known."

How does this all work? I have to make my way along life without my father. He had been my strong supporter. He believed in me and shared with me one day as we were driving along, "Ouida, I don't wat you to be a maid. I want you to get you an office job." He did not live long enough to see, but I never forgot his words.

I was very thankful that I had united with the Salem Institutional Baptist Church. They were the people who had to listen repeatedly to the story of the loss of my father. I had joined the choir and they gave me a song to lead, "The Lord Will Make a Way Somehow." I always wanted to lead a song back at home, but they could never find my key. And the Jones Sisters had such beautiful voices, the rest of us had to sing background. But here, Mrs. Charlesetta Coleman and Ms. Brenda Johnson were able to find my key, it was either B-flat, or E-flat. The words of the song were, "I know the Lord will make a way, yes he will. I know the Lord will make a way, Oh yes he will. He will make a way for you, although you may not see it through. I know the Lord will make a way, Oh yes he will." Were those words really true? Does the Lord make a way somehow? This was the beginning of a new journey. I did not fully comprehend it then, but by faith, I have come this far.

By now working at the hospital, I began to believe that I should be a Nurse. My husband from Houston became a part of my life again, after a time of separation, during the death of my father. He came to live in Dallas. We were a family again, however, with my night shift work hours, he was spending his evening drinking and partying. I later learned that he would sometimes take our young daughter with him to the clubs. This was not the life for me and our daughter. Again the arguing and fights started. We were destined to end our relationship.

After the divorce, it was time to get on with my education. I was inspired by the work of Nurses did in helping to heal the sick. Through researching to find where I could attend school, I applied at El Centro College. Again, I applied for a grant that would help me get through school and was approved. But since I was so involved in the church, and with my limited knowledge of the Nursing career, I did not want to work on weekends. Little did I know the possibilities within nursing, so I did not enroll in the nursing program. I wanted my week-ends off so that I could fully participate in church. One of the statements that was written in my high school memory book was, "a little learning is a dangerous thing." I agree, but it is a limiting thing as well.

As a young woman who sang in the choir, taught Sunday School, was Secretary to the Baptist Training Union, a member of the Missionary Society, totally engaged in the ministry of the local church. I had found my love for God through my work in the local church. I would catch the bus and walk a dangerous path, from Oakland Avenue along Eugene Street to Latimer and Crozier in Dallas, under the cloak of darkness, to get to church. It was frightening, I would walk in the middle of the street and sing songs aloud and until I could see the church. God protected me. Scripture reinforces this, Psalm 145:20, "The Lord watches over all who love him, but all the wicked he will destroy." I am thankful that the Lord watched over me to protect me along the dangerous paths that I have trod.

After my father's death, mother gave me a car and my little girl and I were set. I could not afford an apartment, so I roomed with an elderly couple, Mr. and Mrs. John Collins, who were members of the church and welcomed me as a tenant. There is a word in Scripture that says, "God knows the plans that God has for you, plans to prosper you and to give you a future with hope and not to harm you." Were those mere words for the people of Jeremiah's day, or did they have a modern application?

After leaving the St. Paul Hospital, I went to work for Safeco Insurance Company for about a year and a half. The work was very routine. I was hired as a file clerk. The money was not much better than the hospital, but I now had week-ends off. It was during this time that I met two older women who encouraged me to work hard and they assured me that things would get better for me. Drusilla Davis and Mildred Pope were their names and they were movers and shakers in the company. I was young, but I wanted to be like them because they had more important jobs and of course earned more money.

After about 18 months I left the company and in my search for a job, I was told that the City of Dallas was hiring. I was encouraged to go over and take the Civil Service test for employment. Within three months, I received a call to come for an interview. This was a whole new world of work. I had passed the test and qualified for the position, but the work was different. It required that I type and my skills were at the bottom, but I now had the weekends off so that I could attend worship.

Across the street from the Collins, was the Sister-in-law of my Aunt Louise Jones, Mrs. Annie Mae Jones. Her husband had recently died and she was in a spiritually low state. She was alone and I moved to live with her as a tenant. She was very kind and loved to cook. I can almost smell the aroma of the bread as the wheat would rise in the house. And the delicious fresh caught fish that she would cook. I remember a morning that as I was getting ready to go to work, and the bread was already rising and the smell was overwhelming. And Mrs. Jones said, we are going to have fried fish this evening. However, I told her that I needed to lose weight. When I got home that evening, she had cottage cheese and pears for dinner. I asked, "What happened to the fried fish that we were going to have?" She responded, you said you needed to lose weight." In a matter of minutes, the bread that had been rising all day was in the oven and the fish was in the frying pan. I was so blessed, and loved by a dear Saint who had no children of her own.

Mrs. Jones was a kind woman. We would sit for hours and I would listen to her tell the stories about life with her late husband. How in their younger years, the very house that we were living in was a party place for the young people of her church. She told of parties where the Pastor would show up uninvited and her shoes in her closet would get filled with beer. This had happened long ago, but she loved to share those stories with me. We would laugh and enjoy each other.

Mrs. Jones was later diagnosed with cancer. I would take care of her at night and her sister-in-law would come and stay with her all day. This was a battle that she would not win. She succumbed to cancer a few months later. And because of my willingness to stay with her and care for her at night and tend her needs, I was able to rent the house. By now, I was working as a Clerk for the City of Dallas at the Martin Luther King, Jr., Health Center. I was getting paid a bit more and could now afford to bring my young daughter to live with me. She was attending the Good Street Early Childhood Center on Hatcher Street. I was driving there in the car that my mother had given me.

As a member of the Church, I heard my Pastor, the Reverend J. Whitlow Washington preach to us about being dedicated members of the church. I did not yet know the word, Discipleship. However, we were encouraged to participate in the ministries of the church and to give our tithes. Through many discussions with members of my Sunday School class, who were not willing to make the commitment, I decided that the tithes was to be paid off the top, prior to taxes. And that is what I did. Each Sunday when the tithing period was called, it was my decision to go to the tithing box and give my 10 percent off the top.

Naysayers in the congregations thought that I wanted to make a show of my donations, because the offering was printed in the bulletin. Many discouraging words were spoken about my rationale for giving. As a single young, uneducated woman, the whispers were, "she is giving because she wants to be seen." "She is always at the church because she has nothing else to do." "She is trying to be important." However, it was in the midst of what they were saying about me that God was showing me who I really was. I believe that because I was a tither, God was pouring out extra blessing on me. My income was growing at 25 percent each year. I was being promoted in my employment and I promised the Lord that as I was blessed, I would bless God's church.

One of the greatest tests came on a Sunday that my limited budget had gone as far as it could go. The Pastor called for the tithers to come forward and when I checked my checkbook, I only had enough to pay nursery fees for my daughter. What must I do? I chose to give my tithes to the Lord, realizing that I did not know how I would be able to pay for my daughter's nursery fee. I did it in faith. And "faith is the substance of things hoped for and the evidence of things not seen." I gave my tithes and went home wondering what I would do the next morning. About 3 o'clock my brother called to say that he was on vacation and would I allow my daughter to go with him to visit mother for the week in East Texas. "Yes, she can go," was my response and an answer to prayer. This is the testimony that I share whenever I stand to ask people to walk with me in faith. God is able to work miracles for those who put their trust in Him. Somewhere I heard this quote, "Life is a mystery to be lived and not a problem to be solved," Adriana Trigiani. However, Soren Kierkegaard stated, "Life is not a problem to be solved, but a reality to be experienced." Thank you God, I have attempted to live this life and allow you to lead my life. Though the route has been circuitous, I would take nothing for my journey. My path with God has silenced all of those who only saw and questioned what I did, but did not understand the God who orders the footsteps of those who believe.

The House and a Believer

Upon the death of Mrs. Jones, the Jones house became the property of the younger brother, Rev. Jones. And because I had taken care of his sister, he asked me what I could afford to pay in rent. And I paid that until the time he decided to sell the house. I received the news from the Realtor, Mrs. Mable White. She came by to assess the property. I showed her around the house that my young daughter and I were occupying. As we talked, I learned that she was a member of the Good Street Missionary Baptist Church, a church I was familiar with because we shared in fellowship each Thanksgiving. I shared with her that I was part of the Missionary Department and that we were having a Tea for Women's Day. I asked her to purchase a ticket. She was surprised that I was part of the Missionary Society. At that time, I had never heard the terminology, the "Favor of the Lord." But it was the divine intervention of God that was entering our life circumstances.

After the visit of Mrs. White, I began to think about where my daughter and I would live. I had no savings. I began to search out apartments. And the ones that would fit into my budget were all in South Dallas and not the safest neighborhood. I looked at one on Grand Avenue and the mere surroundings frightened me. It was on the second floor at the back of the building in an impoverished neighborhood. And my daughter and I would be entering alone, at night and I was so scared.

I went home that evening and I was crying because I did not know where we would live. While talking to my next door neighbor, Mrs. Maple Barnes, on the phone and crying, my baby girl said to me, "Mama, sing the Lord Will Make a Way Somehow." I did not understand and not sure that I had even heard the words, "And a little child will lead you," but we lived it. My back was against the wall and the words of the song were strong, and I sang it with power, but did I believe it? "I know the Lord, will make a way, yes He will. He will make a way for you, although you may not see it through. I know the Lord will make a way, yes He will." Did she understand what I was singing? Were those mere melodious words, or does the Lord work in those ways. I thought that I understood what it meant to be a Christian, but I was beginning to understand what it meant to have faith.

Mrs. White came back with a plan for me to purchase the house, because she said, "I believe in you." There is power in having someone believe in you. In about three months after making the application for the house, I had purchased it. God is truly our provider and wants us to put our implicit trust in Him.

It was there in the Salem Institutional Baptist Church, where most of the women who were my age were either in college, or recent graduates, and I was a high school graduate. I knew that I could do better, but I was not financially capable of paying for college. There were in the church a couple of women, who like me had gone to college later in their lives and by their sheer examples, I knew that it was possible for me to do the same. However, my finances were not there. I had a desire to go to school, but many obstacles made it appear to be an impossible feat.

It was during this time that I met Lucy Cain a member of Salem, who had recently graduated from Fisk University and returned home. She was an outgoing, friendly person who played the piano for the Baptist Training Union. After service on Sundays we would go out to places and meet people in Club Arandus, around the corner from where I lived. I was so happy to have a friend in the church who was around my age. So many of the young women in the church who were educated shunned me. But there as something about Lucy that always invited me and we became fast friends. I had a desire for education, but she accepted me as a friend.

My Career in City Government Begins

In June 1971 my career began with the City of Dallas. I was hired as a Clerk at the Martin Luther King, Jr. Center, before the buildings were actually built. I was hired to work in the Health Department and my office was located in a house on Pennsylvania Avenue. It was not long before the new Health Building became a reality and we moved there. As a young woman who had been reared in the country, I needed to get my bearing and learn to use this new IBM typewriter that was on my desk. I was working in an office and my duties were to welcome in the patients, type simple information and escort the patients that were to be seen to the appropriate offices.

In order for us to move up within City Government, we had to take tests. I kept my eye open for the positions that I could qualify for and was satisfied with the income that I was earning. Additionally, I was only a few miles from home. After my father's death, my mother gave me his car and that was reliable transportation for me to get to work and to church. I was moving up.

During the summer of 1972, I began to date the Director of the Baptist Training Union, Brother John C. Lee, Jr. He was a few years my senior and had never been married. He asked me to marry him and I said yes. One of the things that I told him was that I wanted to go to college. His promise to me was, "when we get married, I will help you go to school." He was a man that was financially stable. He owned his own home, and had worked for the U.S. Postal Service for many years. He took me to places that I had never been exposed to and took me shopping in stores that I could not afford to buy from. He said all of the right words that appealed to me, and even supported me in my quest for education. Yes was my response and we were married in November.

Dating was not an easy experience, our work schedules were different, mine 8-5 and his 3-11. There were times that he would come to my house at midnight and want to sit and talk, and I would want to go to bed, because I needed to be at work at 8 a.m. We shared Sunday worship, Sunday

School, lunches after church and Baptist Training Union in the evening. We enjoyed movies occasionally and he was very kind to my little daughter. He took me to my first Dallas Cowboy Football Games and shopping for clothes to wear to that game. This new man was showing me a life that I had not experienced and there was the promise of a college education. We were married in November of 1972 and immediately things changed. When I said, "I am ready to go to school," he said, "you should have done that before we got married." "But you promised me." No matter of arguing was going to change his mind, nor was I willing to accept defeat of my dream of a college education.

I can admit now that those words so disappointed me, but there was something within me that said, you can do it. That reminds me of the words of one of the songs that I would learn in the church. "Something within me that holdeth the reins. Something within me that banishes pain. Something within me, I cannot explain. All that I know, there is something within." Perhaps it was the struggles of life and the way that God has blessed me that kept me focused and successful that made me continue my quest for education. There were two women in the Church, Mrs. Clearone Davis and her sister, Mrs. Margaret Walker who graduated with their Masters' degrees from Southern Methodist University. And they were friendly, outgoing and encouraging. They told me, "Weet, you can do it!" I believed them, and I am going to give it all that I have to get that education.

I was now working for the City of Dallas, as a Clerk. Working among so many educated women in the workplace and within the church, and embedded in my DNA, was a college educated woman. Now was not the time, nor did I have the income, so I settled in as a wife, working mother and dedicated church woman. Yet, the dream of college and my association with women who like me, had gone to college later in life, I dreamed. I was studying the word of the Lord and believed it philosophically, yet, as I sang the gospel songs and began to trust God with my discipleship and stewardship, I believed the Lord would make a way somehow for me to go to college too.

I continued to test and promote within the City of Dallas. Every Department was like working for a new company. I promoted to a Clerk 6 to the Equipment Services Department. Later I promoted to a Clerk 8 and became the Safety Officer of the Department. I took every Personnel Course that was offered and became the Equal Opportunity Officer for Equipment Services. Since we had numerous cars that were being driven by employees, I requested that I take the Defensive Driving Instructors Certification Couse. After approval, I added that skill to my resume. I was hired by the Street and Sanitation Department as Safety Officer for the Sanitation Division. Later I tested and qualified to become Administrative Assistant with the Dallas Water Utilities. My responsibilities were to edit the departmental newsletter, the News and Vews. From South Dallas, I was now hired at new City Hall. All along this journey, I was putting my whole trust in God and working diligently within my faith community.

Studying the Bible has the potential to teach those who are open to living in accordance to the will of God. I am not speaking of perfectionism, because I made more than my share of mistakes. In many ways, I must have disappointed God with my behavior. However, like David in Psalm 51, I was willing to confess to God my mistakes and to ask forgiveness and leave my sins in the hands of the Lord. Uncertain of how Philippians 4:13 caught my attention, but to hear and believe, "I can do all things through Christ who strengtheneth me." All things? I can do? Belief and trust is God is foundational to the journey of faith. I read the word of the Lord in Scripture, I wondered about its truth, I trusted in the Word. It began with my singing the Gospel songs, and stepping out in faith. The interesting thing about how God enlightens us, tithing was a big part of the journey. Malachi 3:10, "Bring ye all of the tithes into the storehouse, that there may be meat in mine house, and prove me now herewith saith the Lord of hosts, if I will not open you the windows of heaven and pour you out a blessing, that there shall not be room enough to receive it." I tried it. It works. God blessed me phenomenally when I began to tithe. That was all that I had that I could do. Could it be possible that God would bless me to go to school? Yes. God did.

Our family began to grow with the addition of our daughter Libbie. She was the Church's baby. Everyone wanted to hold her. She was beautiful, fluffy and smiled easily. My time was consumed with motherly duties of caring for the children, cooking, and sewing, which was my past time making garments for the entire family. Our son John III was our third child completing our family. Regina began piano lessons and along with the activities of the Church, I become involved in the Parents and Teachers Association at the elementary school. As Libbie grew and began to walk, along comes our baby John. He is not as friendly as Libbie and does not want anyone to hold onto him, but his mother. Now there are three and since my husband works nights, we spent many evening traveling to the church together. The kids are in the children's choir, dance school on Saturday, Cub Scouts, Brownies and Girl Scouts, piano lessons and PTA. Our lives were consumed.

As a Sunday School Teacher and Departmental Superintendent of Sunday School, I enjoyed the challenge of studying the word of the Lord. I want to be assured that I was teaching the lessons with authority, therefore, time was spent in commentaries, other books. My commitment as a teacher is always to be as accurate as possible. Additionally, as member of the Missionary Society, I was elected President at the age of 31. The women had worked with me as their Vice President for 3 years and they elected me to lead them. I was honored and humbled by their vote. We were no longer a group locked within the church, we visited Nursing Homes, took lessons, sang, made coverlets for the women and served them refreshment. We were a great team. God blessed our work, our finance and the support to the church and the community.

We raised lots of funds and our support was unbelievable. One of the most memorable fundraisers was an idea that I dreamed and the women of the Church supported. It was called the Debutantes for Christ. I wanted the girls in the church to understand that because their parents were not of the "Society" groups they could nevertheless be Debutantes. It was the intent of the Missionary Department to raise funds so that we could attend the National Baptist Convention. I shared the idea with the Circles of the Department and each of the women selected one girl. The girl was to raise funds and present a talent and a faith statement. Each girl was to be escorted by a male youth. The affair became elaborate. Girls were going to be dressed in Debutante dresses and the Boys were to wear tuxedos. Each the circles supported a girl and on the evening of the event excitement was running high, because I, as President, had pledged to win the contest.

Each of the participants presented their talent – some dramatist, piano maestros, soloists. Afterward, each debutante so beautifully dressed in white dresses and holding a single carnation, strolled down the aisle with her escort. The photographer was present and took individual pictures. Finally, it was time to crown the Debutante for Christ Pageant winner. I was holding the crown in my hand as the Finance Chair announced the money. As President, I was to crown the winner. Holding my breath through the third runner up, the second runner up and the winner. My daughter, Regina Lee with more than $2240. I shakily placed the crown on her head. We had raised overall, $10,000 for the church budget.

Our major project was to send representatives to the National Baptist Convention, and to do renovation work on the Women's restroom. We supported the work of the Youth, taking them to a National Conference for Christian Education in Indianapolis, Indiana. A delegation of the Missionary Department attended the National Convention in Florida and was part of the Historic delegation that elected a new President, Dr. T. J. Jimerson in 1982. We truly came to understand that when people of faith work together, there is nothing that cannot be accomplished.

Life deals you many different challenges, and though school never left my mind, I continued my work within the church, loving every minute of it. Marriage gave me the opportunity to travel across the states, especially with the National Congress for Christian Educators with a team from our church and the National Baptist Convention, USA Incorporated. We would tour the cities and attempt to see the highlights. We attended the Dallas Cowboys Football games, we were both fans. Those were great days, attending the Opera at Fair Park Music Hall, where my loving husband had to interpret for me what was happening. Traveling via car to Los Angeles, CA where I met some of his family. Attending Disneyland and Knottsberry Farm, Universal Studios and Chinatown. Another year we traveled to beautiful San Franciso, CA crossing the Golden Gate Bridge, and visiting Muir Woods Park, Fisherman's Wharf and Telegraph Hill.

The word of the Lord intrigued me. I loved to hear the word proclaimed and heard so many approaches to preaching. Two of my favorites were Dr. Frederick G. Sampson of Detroit, MI and Dr. E. V. Hill of Los Angeles, CA. Two very different approaches, but both of which claimed my attention. And one of my role models was Dr. Mary O. Ross National President of the Women's Auxiliary. Dr. Ross was a powerful woman in the convention and invited powerful women to accompany her on her journey. Though I was never on stage with her, in my heart and spirit, she showed me the power, humility and prestige that women could hold within the church.

As President of the Missionary Society, and one who loved to proclaim the teachings of the Scriptures, I was a participant for many of the Model Mission programs and Annual Women's Days in the city of Dallas. We were not allowed in the pulpits, but that did not prohibit our proclamation of the word of the Lord. We had a story to tell to the nation and it was a word that empowered the women of the church, not to take control, but to walk alongside of the men of the church. The Missionary Departments across the city of Dallas gave me the opportunity to bring full expression to the word of the Lord. Almost every week, I was a speaker for one of the many Dallas Churches. I had to study hard because when I was teaching, it was important to me that I would be accurate in my teaching. As one who had been an Orator since elementary school and with the opportunity to watch women on the National Baptist Convention stage, I felt equipped. Along with hearing the messages as preached by power preachers, i.e. Dr. Frederick G. Sampson and Dr. E. V. Hill along with many others, I was inspired and wanted to inspire others to know the truth of Gods word as understood by a woman. I loved hearing the preaching of the Gospel, but I always created my own messages and attempted to make them relevant.

Education

My journey of education began in the El Centro Junior College. I would take classes there for several years. I later began to take classes at Cedar Valley College while working as a Clerk with the Martin Luther King Jr. Center in South Dallas. The challenge would be greater now because we now we had three children, Regina, Libbie and John. The Cedar Valley college was near my home and I would attend classes in the evenings. I asked my husband to change his shift and be home at night with the kids so that I could attend class. He was unwilling to do so, therefore, I attempted attending at night leaving the kids at home alone. I shall always remember the night that I came home and all three of my children were sitting on the sofa leaning on each other, because they had heard a noise. It so saddened me that I finished the semester and dropped out. They were babies, but I knew that they would grow up.

When I was able to afford a baby sitter to stay with my children at night, I began school again. This would be the time that I would complete my Associates Degree through the Dallas County Community College District in Applied Arts and Sciences. I hired Heather Williams, a teenager to babysit my children. I would prepare their meals, put them on the plates and pick her up to sit with the children. When I returned from class, I would take her home and come home to study.

I graduated from Cedar Valley College in 1985, and the Salem Institutional Baptist Church celebrated me with the presentation of a plaque. I was honored, but this was the beginning of my studies. In January 1986 I enrolled in a program at Dallas Baptist University that could grant me 30 credit hours based upon my Career experience. By now, I had been working for the City of Dallas for more than 15 years. I sought to take every Civil Service examination possible and had promoted from a Clerk 4 in 1971 to an Administrative Assistant 10.

I did not have the luxury of being a full-time student, I was a parent on a journey to success. And it was with the help of the Lord that I had the strength to persevere along the journey. My favorite Scripture was one that I found through my studies, "I can do all things through Christ who strengtheneth me, Philippians 4:13 I never let go of the hand of the Lord. And may I add that this was not an easy path, there were challenges all along the path. But I have learned that God is able to do "exceedingly and abundantly more than we could ever ask or imagine."

I continued to serve as President of the Missionary Department of the Church. And I was a sought after speaker for not only the Baptist, but the Second Cumberland Presbyterian, Methodist and some Pentecostal Churches. My first invitation to the Presbyterian Church was to speak for their National meeting in Nashville, TN. You cannot imagine how humbled I was to be invited and flown to Tennessee by the Denomination. I arrived early in the morning and rested in one of their guest rooms until it was time for me to speak. Later that evening, I flew back to Dallas Lovefield. Little did I know that that would be the beginning of my trips to share the word of the Lord.

It is time to remove the veil. More than 25 years ago, I clearly hear the call to go and proclaim the Word of the Lord. It was a free and easy time. My messages were given mostly to women, on 5th Sunday afternoon programs, Model Missions and occasionally a Sunday morning message. Oh yes, there were workshops, seminars and women's conferences on Saturday mornings. And I must not forget my obligatory work with Women's Missionary meetings on Monday nights and Sunday School classes and never forget the Christian Education Workshops.

At the time, I was invited most often to speak with Women's Missionary meetings. And as a mother who was busy with my work in the church and attempting to be a loving mother I got the surprise of my life. I learned that my 16 year old daughter was pregnant. I was working for the City of Dallas and when speaking, I would often share statistics about teen-age pregnancy in my messages. My daughter was now a statistic. I believe even to this day that this was an attempt by Satan to keep me silent. It was painful for me to learn this news and I cried so many tears. As her mother, I hurt because I knew this would not be an easy task, to complete her high school education and then go to college. However, one night in the midst of my tears and hurt, God reminded me that I had been forgiven for all of my sins and shortcomings. And forgiven people become compassionate people. I dried my eyes and never cried again. And rather than attempt to hide the story from others, I took it on and shared our story as a testimony to other women. Standing with my daughter in many oppositional places and holding her in support and with the understanding of the unconditional love of Jesus Christ. It was my belief that I was to keep silent and not share the story, but my God urged me to share the story to help other mothers who may have been challenged in the same way. My daughter was a musician who played for the Sunday School and the Baptist Training Union. Some of the older adults insisted that she not play for the church because she might be a model for other youth. But with her gifts, she was hired by another church as their musician. Proverbs 18:16 "A gift opens the way and ushers the giver into the presence of the great," and her gift has made room for her and she has been playing for churches now more than 37 years.

When the baby, Shanel was born, she became like my own child. She was loved with an unconditional love by the members of our church. And she attended many church meetings with me until she was six year old, she then went to live with her mother. We now had another teen daughter who became pregnant at the age of 16, Libbie. She needed our help. As a leader in the church, I felt particularly challenged, but again could see that Satan was challenging our family. But again I shared the testimonies with people who like our family was going through struggles. The Bible tells us in Luke 22:31. "And the Lord said, Simon, Simon, behold, Satan hath desired to have you that he may sift you as wheat." That could have been the end of my ministry. I felt like a complete failure until I remembered these words. Studying God's word, I found that his words with prayer were an anchor to my life. He knew that I was courageous and wanted to break me. To shut me down. He did not want me to tell the victorious stories of faith to women. Women who would come up to me after the Women's meetings and whisper in my ear, "Thank you for sharing your testimony, I was teaching Sunday School, but when my grandbaby was born, I was too ashamed to go back." My friends, when we stop, we give Satan the victory. We have to stand in faith, although we often do not know where the Lord is leading us. Remember God knows the plans that He has for you, plans to prosper you and to give you a future with hope and not to harm you.

Regina graduated Booker T. Washington School for the Performing Arts and went to college that fall, attending North Texas State University. Shanel grew up as a beautiful young lady, graduating Skyline High School in 2003 and Jarvis Christian College in 2007. Libbie had a bouncing baby boy whom she named Lexion. She decided to go to the school for pregnant teens where she earned her best GPA ever. She graduated South Oak Cliff High School and went off to Prairie View A & M University. Her son Lexion graduated Lancaster High School in 2011 and attended Lon Morris College and graduated Texas College in 2018. The success of my children and their parents is based in the love and nurture shown them throughout their lives.

My scope of work was filled with my commitment to my Lord and Savior Jesus Christ, being a dedicated wife and mother of three young children. Teaching the word of God to my sisters in the faith and encouraging others to come along and learn of my Lord and Savior Jesus Christ. The more I studied the word of the Lord, the more I felt compelled to believe the truths of the Bible. Particularly drawn to the stories of women and the way that I heard them proclaimed from pulpits, always the women were culprits. Women were always at fault. And the more I heard the Easter Resurrection story of Jesus and the encounter with Mary at the tomb, more questions arose in my mind. There was the desire to know more. To be drawn into the story when Jesus called Mary, by name "Go to my brothers and sisters and tell them, I am going up to my Father and your Father, to my God and your God. Mary Magdalene left and announced to the disciples, I've see the Lord."[1] Did she just go and tell? Just once? Then why do I have to keep silent?

After hearing me deliver a message to a group of Missionary Women at a Banquet in 1991. I sat down at the head table and observing the obnoxious look of the host pastor, my heart sank. Though the assembled group was ecstatic about the message, I felt unwelcomed. Later that evening, my husband said to me, "women are not supposed to preach," to which my quick response was, "I can do whatever my God calls me to do."

Did my journey begin immediately? No. Fear held me captive. I talked about my call with friends. My heart was so filled with the Word of the Lord. I could develop a sermon from any topic. Yet, it was about fear, and what it would feel like to be alone. I became silent. Unwilling to talk about it because I felt trapped. If I responded to God's call would I be divorced? If I kept silent and unresponsive to God, what would happen? I shared my thoughts with the Reverend Dr. Michael Wayne Walker, a young man who had grown up in Salem, but was now a Pastor in Brockton, Massachusetts. He was one the son of Johnny and Margaret Walker and when I shared with him that I felt that I was called of God to preach, he asked me what I was going to do about it? I shared my fears of the loss of my husband and that I would be put out of the church as other women before me. His question to me, "would you rather obey God or man?" "Wow." That was a powerful question, I had to think about that. And his further advice was, and when you go to school, go to Perkins School of Theology at Southern Methodist University, they will teach you how to think." Admittedly, I did not understand what he meant, but overtime, I have grown in the process of ministry and have concluded that his advice was excellent. As a woman, there were many times that my call would be challenged, but a thinker knows how to respond.

The journey continued with my invitations to speak on special occasions. My heart would be filled with joy as I penned the messages and had the opportunity to share them with others. The Bible was filled

---

[1] The Common English Bible. John 20:17b-18a. Copyright 2011.

with adventure and I wanted to share what I was learning as I studied the Scripture. During my time of discernment, I wrote a course entitled, Image Building for Youth. It was a six hour interactive message to the youth based upon Scripture and giving the youth the opportunity to give feedback. And while on a visit to New Orleans, Louisiana, I had the opportunity to share the teachings with two different churches. I was hopeful that they would invite me back to teach the course. However, in a strange set of circumstances, the word came back to Dallas, Texas that I was there preaching.

It was not my intent to stand against the system. I was willing to "bootleg" and "stay home" and connected denominationally, and keep silent. My mind was made up to never discuss the topic again. Through my ultra-conservative denomination, the word spread like wild-fire. She is preaching.

Prior to my trip to New Orleans, I had been invited by the Christian Educators to come and teach the youth, I was banned without notice. Prepared, but banned. Even though I questioned why I was not allowed to teach, there were no answers. Finally on the day of the event, I was called into a closed door meeting, and questioned, "Have you been called to preach? Tears welled up in my eyes and while clutching the bible in my hands, it was as if God spoke through the cover, "whoever is ashamed of me and my words in this unfaithful generation, the Human One will be ashamed of that person when he comes to the Father's glory with the holy angels.²"

Have you the feeling of being crushed underneath the weight of one who is called to love and support you? Do you know the feeling of an alternate, unplanned journey? Have you wounds in your heart because you have felt abandoned? Yes, I know all of those feelings, but my call was from a caring, loving, real and the original Promise-keeper, Jesus Christ.

It is important for you to know that I was still working for the City of Dallas. After several years in Dallas Water Utilities, I was promoted to the Dallas City Council Office. I was Council Assistant to Councilman Charles Tandy, M.D. I was very proud and humbly served in this office. I was a citizen of the community and understood when the citizens complained. I also was a veteran employee who had worked for many of

---

² The Common English Bible. Mark 8:38. Copyright 2011.

the departments of the city. I had contacts in almost every department and when there were needs, I could get immediate action. However, that was not the way that the City wanted to operate.

Dr. Charles Tandy was the head of Anesthesiology at Methodist Dallas Hospital. This was a very exciting career opportunity. I had the opportunity of sharing with the community residents on behalf of my Council Member. And during our down time in the office, members of the staff would share their International travels. I was the only one who had not been outside of the United States. One of the Assistants was sharing the advertisement of the Annual Mobil Classic Parade that was held on January 1st each year. She offered us tickets to watch from the stands that would be placed in front of City Hall. I requested four so that I could take my children with me.

Each year at the Parade, a grand prize would be given away, we only had to place our names on ballots and they would be placed in one of the Gifford-Hill concrete mixing trucks. One name would be drawn for the winner of the grand prize that year, a trip for four via American Airlines to anywhere on the Continent of Europe. As I sat in the stands, I mumbled to myself, "I am going to be the winner." I asked my son to go and get ballots for me. He brought me back eleven. I filled them out and told him to take them to the young lady and we watched her as she climbed the ladder to drop them in the truck. This time I mumbled, "Our ticket will not be drawn." However, the next morning when I arrived at City Hall, the Council Assistant who gave me the tickets said, "Ouida did you know that you were the grand prize winner?" "What?" I screamed. The whole office came to see what I was screaming about, and soon the word spread over City Hall. In my own smug way, "We are going to Europe." There were a few blackout dates, but we were going. I made arrangements through a travel agent for room and board, and our three children, Regina in college and Libbie and John were in elementary school, but we were flown Business Class to London Gatwick Airport, free. Wow! God really does give us the desire of our hearts. There was the Changing of the Guards at Buckingham Palace, and Big Ben, the River Thames and Stratford upon Avon, the burial place of Henry Wadsworth Longfellow, Anne Hathaways's Thatched Cottage, Liverpool and Stonehenge. Unbelievable!

Do you know the one? Quotes from the Bible encourage me on this journey, "Be strong! Be fearless! Don't be afraid and don't be scared by your enemies, because the Lord your God is the one who marches with you. He won't let you down, and he won't abandon you,[3]" Deuteronomy 31:6 (CEV) Thank you God for your affirmation. I am aware that the Scripture is about Joshua entering into leadership upon the death of Moses. Fully aware that this is Old Testament Scripture, and it is spoken to Joshua. But, if one believes in the Scripture, one learns that God's word is not limited by generations, or gender, and provides a foundation on which to stand. And even more, the one who is walking without support and affirmation is compelled to walk by faith and not by sight, clinging rigidly to the Scripture. And the Bible records in Hebrews 13:8, "Jesus Christ is the same yesterday, today and forever.[4]

The year 1987 was a paramount year for me in education. It had been 20 years since my high school graduation at Mayflower High School of Tatum, Texas. In May I would get my Bachelor's degree from Dallas Baptist University. Regina was in her first year at North Texas State and my obligation to her education was to pay my half of her expenses which included room and board, books. John would pay the other half. In addition, I had to pay my final semester for classes at DBU. I knew that I had no money. When it was time to go back for my final semester, I could not see my way. I shall always remember Ester Louise Williams who said, "Go anyway." How could I go when I had no money? I shared my story with a colleague at work. Her name was Kim Ardila and she was over the tuition reimbursement in the Human Resources Department for the City of Dallas. She reminded me, "Ouida, you have just finished a semester and you have a $500 check that will be coming to you in a few weeks. I will write a letter for you and you can take that with you."

When I arrived at DBU, I wanted to get the Financial Aid Department to approve the letter, but they told me to get in line and pick up my classes. I was so nervous, but I did what they told me. I picked up my final classes and when I got to the payment station, I was asked, "How do you plan to pay for these classes?" I was so nervous, I could not speak. I simply handed the paper to the staff and the manager read the letter and stamped

---

[3] The Common English Bible. Deuteronomy 31:6. Copyright, 2011.
[4] The Common English Bible. Hebrews 13:8. Copyright 2011.

"Approved." You cannot imagine how I felt. God was with me, I was not alone.

Heartfelt memories flood my soul that evening in May 1987 as we were told, you have already met all of the credentials for graduation, turn those tassels to the other side. We walked across the campus down a slight hill to the auditorium. The door must have been 10 feet tall and my head was all the way to the top. I had graduated with a Bachelor's Degree from Dallas Baptist University. And it was in the graduation ceremony where I observed the other students being "hooded" that I knew one was in my future. I thought that it would be a degree in Public Administration since I was a city employee. But then I remembered my conversation with Rev. Dr. Walker, get a degree in something that you can make a difference in the lives of others.

What was it that would make a difference in the lives of others? I had long since come to the understanding that life is not just about ones' selfish desires. And it is not just about making money, or being promoted by others. It was about making a difference in this world. In self-reflection, I have learned that God was truly ordering my footsteps. What was it that I was most passionate about? I believed that things should be done in "just" ways, but I did not feel that had worked very well for me. I was always speaking up for justice, but others always seemed to get the benefits. What was God teaching me? To keep silent and not care about others? The Black Man's Plea for Justice spoken long ago deeply influenced my thinking. Yet, we live in a world that is slow to make changes. God was leading me and calling me to tell the stories about Jesus who always stood for justice, grace and mercy, but so often misunderstood. Simultaneously, my success in life had taught me that when God is with you, He is more than the world against you. Who knew the challenges that I would face in ministry? The pushback. The deception. The discrimination, and insults. But simultaneously the blessings, the peace, the revolutionary love that would transform my life. God who not only knew my name, but who would forgive all of my sins and trespasses and teach me how to put together the stories in ways that others would be willing to try this God for themselves.

While still employed by the City of Dallas, I began my studies at the Perkins School of Theology at SMU in the fall of 1991. Most Master's degrees required 30 to 45 hours, but a Master's of Divinity required 81 hours and I would be a part time evening student. I was laterally transferred to the Housing Department in 1991, just in time to begin my journey as a student of Theology. Wow!! Little did I know that God was ordering my footsteps.

After acknowledging my call to ministry to the Galilee Griggs Memorial District Association of the Baptist Church, I was stripped of all leadership. Therefore, I decided to focus my attention on graduate school. I thought that I could stay in the Salem Church, but one of the women told me that I should leave because I was never going to be accepted there. And some of my colleagues at Perkins asked me why I was staying there. That was a question that I had to answer. I was still afraid that if I left the church I would lose my husband. However, his words to me were, "If God called you, you have to go, but I will not be going with you." Within weeks after those words were spoken to me, I joined the St. Luke Community United Methodist Church, in October 1991, under the leadership of the Rev. Dr. Zan W. Holmes, Jr. He told me, "Ouida, you do not have to leave your church, I will still let you come here and preach." I expressed thanks, but told him that I was a Sunday School Teacher and my whole class had abandoned me. I said whatever I did as leadership was questioned. He then said to me, "you are welcomed to St. Luke and I will never question your call."

I found a home at St. Luke, however, the rules of the United Methodist Church mandated that I would not be able to preach for a year. I understood. I joined the Women's Choir, United Methodist Women, and taught grades 1-3 Sunday School. The class grew phenomenally that the class was divided into three classes. I attended Wednesday night Prayer and Praise every week and sang and prayed. This was a new form of worship, and I had much to learn, but with great teachers, Rev. Chauncey Neely was Liturgist and taught the congregation about the Christian Calendar year, the changing of the colors of banners and their meaning. And I had a front row seat in the 8 a.m. and 10 a.m. worship, I was there to learn and Pastor Zan was a Preachers' preacher. Ministry was exciting and I had to attend New Member Orientation, Pastor Zan was the teacher.

The St. Luke Church was home for many seminary students and Pastor Zan would meet with us in his home once monthly. Although I had to wait for a year before I could preach, I was invited to share with the Preachers monthly. One of the preachers who was attending the St. Luke Church at the time was from Florida and he was in Chaplain Ministry at Parkland Hospital. His family still lived in Florida, yet he had an appointment to the St. James and Haven Chapel United Methodist Churches in the Sherman-McKinney District. He asked me if I would preach for him on Sunday and I was thrilled. He said, "I know the rules of the Methodist Church, but I know when a person has been called to preach, they do not want to wait a whole year before they get to preach." When I preached the Haven Chapel Church paid me, but the St. James Church told me that I would have to get my pray from the Pastor when he returned. Some of the members of the St. James church told me that I might be their Pastor someday. I thanked them and said that would be wonderful. About two week later, the Pastor told me that he had a car accident and asked if I would go and preach for him again. Excitedly, I responded yes. The next month, the Pastor advised that he had purchased tickets to go home and see his family once each month and wanted to know if I would be willing to fill in for him. Of course I was excited about doing so. But by March the Pastor shared that he was returning to Florida and wanted me to take over the churches. Though I had only been in the UMC a short time, I knew there was a process to making this happen.

Even though the Pastor was willing to leave the two churches in my hands, I thought I needed to consult with Pastor Holmes. I shared that I could use the money because seminary was very expensive and I was paying all of the debt alone. Rev. Holmes advised that he would speak to the District Superintendent and see if they wanted me to continue to serve the appointment. This was an unusual circumstance since I was a student in seminary, and was a candidate minister with the Dallas South District, and the church was in the Sherman-McKinney District. However, with the support of Rev. Holmes, the Sherman-McKinney District Superintendent, Dr. Jim Pledger gladly accepted me into their District. I was the only person of color appointed to the District.

It is important for me to share that at the time of my beginning this journey, I was full-time employed by the City of Dallas, in the Department of Housing and Neighborhood Services. Getting through Seminary was no easy feat. It took me 5 years, at night and every term, including summer and January two week -term. But thank God I made it. I have to share that Dr. Virgil Howard was my Intern professor. He would come to Sherman to meet with my Intern Committee. He shared with them that they should come to my graduation because I was going to receive a special award. I was much too busy to apply for any awards, or even to be aware of them. My classes were at night, I worked a job from 8:15 to 5:15 Monday through Fridays, and spent Friday night through Sunday evening in Sherman. And I mention that I was keeping my grandson Lexion while my daughter Libbie was in Prairie View A & M University for a year.

The membership in the St. James Church was approximately 11 people and the Haven Chapel Church had a constituency of 8 members, all were adults and most of them elderly. Even though the Salem Institutional Baptist Church had over 800 members, and St. Luke several thousands, these small churches did not frighten me. I had been raised in small membership country churches. I was appointed as a "Supply Pastor" until June and then a Local Pastor at Annual Conference, June 1993. Since I had not completed Local Pastors' training, a retired Elder in the Sherman McKinney District would come each first Sunday and bless the Communion elements.

This was one of the most exciting times of my life, I was going to be a Pastor…of two churches. I was a friendly person who loved people and got to know the members in new ways. I lived 75 miles south of the Sherman Church and it was necessary for me to do meetings with them. Therefore, on Saturday morning, I would make my way to the churches for local church meetings. Since I had attended Church Council meetings at St. Luke, I was somewhat familiar with the nature of these meetings. We listened to reports and made ministry plans. I wanted to see the two churches grow. The St. James church was a family sized church and the members were family. They had their methods, and attempted to fill all of the leadership positions among themselves. My question to them was, were there any children in the church because I had never seen any. Mrs. Pauline Neblett, a loving, dedicated saint of the church advised that there was the McKee Family and they had children. Not long after, the McKess children, all five of them between two sisters showed up at church. I was so delighted.

Wash McKee was the oldest of the children and it was not long before he had recruited all of his friends and we began to have Baptisms within the congregation. They formed the choir and their aunts, Andrea and Malinda became our young adults. Another key to our growth was Phiebie Hutchins who came to work with me each week-end. She was the songtress and a Lay Speaker who helped to bring life to the St. James Church. It was not long before we had the United Methodist Women functioning and were host to community outreach programs that brought together women across denominations.

Simultaneously, the Haven Chapel Church began to grow because the members of the church began to invite back to worship persons who had once been members and other unchurched friends. Mrs. Cora Lee Bell was Lay Leader and was key to bringing the Church back together again. Her sister Mrs. Frances Ware played the most beautiful music. We were blessed with some faithful members who also had family that were not currently attending worship. Mrs. Cora Lee Bell, Administrative Council Chair, who became my most ardent supporter. Ms. Rhonda Williams was chair of Finance and Ms. Hattie Powell joined within a year of my arrival and became part of the foundation of the church. She was part of a large family and had friends who eventually united with us. Along with other visionary members Mrs. Viola Walker, Mrs. Garrett, Mrs. Alpha Jordan, Mrs. Frances Ware, who became our musician. They wanted the Haven Chapel Church to survive and supported every visionary idea that God placed in my head.

I continued my employment with the City of Dallas on a full-time basis and worked hard on the week-end to build the St. James/Haven Chapel Charge. As a full-time student at Perkins, my life was totally consumed, because in additional to the week-end church, there were Sunday afternoon fellowships with churches in the area. And as a person who commits wholeheartedly to my work, hospital and home visitations on the week-end. My weekends were extremely exhausting. I would drive to Sherman and Denison on Saturdays, attend the Church Council meetings, which were quite often filled with arguments, visit the sick and homebound, drive back to Dallas on Saturday evenings. Cook and clean the house and prepare our meal for Sunday dinner. Rise at 5:30 to dress and drive to Denison in order to host Sunday school at Haven Chapel at 9 a.m., preach the 10 a.m. worship. Race to Sherman for the 11:45 a.m. worship, preach and rush back to Dallas so that my family could share dinner by 2 p.m. I think that I wanted to prove to my husband that I could do it all… Superwoman.

One of my first outings in Sherman was a fellowship with the Payne Chapel African Methodist Episcopal Church. It was a Federated Choirs Sunday and as I was about to enter the service, I was approached by a gentleman by the name of Ron Clark. He introduced himself to me and shared that he was running for the office of State Representative for the area. When I shared that I was a new Pastor in the area, he asked if I could help him to share a few words during the service. At the end of the service, I shared with the Pastor who allowed me to introduce him. Who knew that because of that introduction, I would be invited to the State Capital in Austin, TX to open a meeting of the House of Representatives? Servanthood pays dividends.

Another favorable move of the Lord occurred when during the first months, as I followed my congregation around, we were invited to the Friendly Church of God in Christ. The Superintendent invited me to share the pulpit. He remarked, "I have never done this before, but if God called you, who am I to stand against you. You are welcomed to join me and the rest of the Ministers in the pulpit." Wow, look at God!

Throughout this time, I was a Perkins Seminary student I did not have a computer. I also failed to mention that I was not proficient on the computer. Since I was a fulltime employee I did have access to computers after hours. There were many papers to complete and I did not have the funds to pay for my work. A young coworker, Ms. Joyce Rhyan, Urban Planner from the state of Tennessee, stood over my shoulders and taught me how to write and save my documents. She was an Urban Planner for the Department of Housing in the City of Dallas, very businesslike and committed to her task of Planning in Dallas. When I told her that I did not understand how to use computers, she took the time to spend with me and taught me the basics. I cannot recall the nights that I would stay at City Hall, typing my papers for seminary. After staff left and the only lights on in the building were the safety lights, I worked long and hard because I did not own my own computer. However, when one has goals, determination and the will to do, hard work pays off.

Seminary was challenging and writing of the papers was the most difficult. I tried, but my grades were always low. Since I was at St. Luke, I spoke with several of my colleagues about writing, all of whom were succeeding with flying colors, but their answer was, "I am doing well." One night I spoke with a student whom I knew was very intelligent, a lawyer by profession, who was also in seminary. She shared that her grades were good and I shared that I did not understand what I was doing wrong. She shared with me, "I am going to allow you to see one of my papers, but if someone learns about this I will never do it again." I swore that what I needed was a pattern. I did my readings, but after reading her paper, I instantly saw the difference. It went back to what Rev. Michael Walker had spoken to me earlier, they were there to teach me how to think, I was simply regurgitating what they had said. I was not reflecting upon what they had said and offering my own thoughts. After reading her paper, I had it. I was keenly aware that I had come from a high school that did not have a complete set of Encyclopedias. I knew that it was a segregated separate but equal country school. But I began to hear the tapes playing in my head, "they can never take from you what you have," Mrs. Irene Johnson. And "Isaac, you're cream of the crop and cream always rises to the top," Algie Harkless. Yes there were students who were much smarter than I was, but I had a God on my side who had taught me through word and deed that, "nothing is impossible with God," and "I can do all things through Christ who strengthens me," the Apostle Paul. May I tell you that I graduated seminary, working full-time, Pastoring, part-time, as a wife, mother and grandmother, with an 83 average. God is good all the time.

On my last semester of Seminary, I had signed up for a day class that met once weekly. It was my plan to take vacation time each week for the hours that I would need to be away. However, we had an Interim Department Director who said he would not approve my time off and that I should drop the class. When I begged, he said that I should have asked him before I enrolled in the class. He had no idea that I was a faithful follower of Jesus Christ, one who prayed all throughout the day. I did not drop the class, but did not know how I was going to finish my final course. Possibly a week before the class was to begin, the City Manager hired a beautiful smiling woman as the new Director. I approached her immediately and explained my situation, she said, "Ouida I applaud you and will in no way stand in your way. Take the class." Faith sometimes makes us stand in some frightful places, but ultimate trust in God works on our behalf.

It was graduation day, and as we gathered in the fellowship hall of the Highland Park United Methodist Church, we were all ecstatic. We made our way into the sanctuary where hundreds of family members had gathered to see us graduate. I have to share that the shoes that I was wearing that day had a piece of metal sticking out of the bottom and I could not afford to purchase a new pair. I was not worried because I was walking with a crowd. But when I was called out to receive the Karlis Fadley award, I had to walk alone, and my I tell you I could hear the tic-tic of the metal against the sanctuary floor. I accepted the award and returned to my seat. I was excited about getting hooded and stepped forth proudly as my name was called and stooped to get hooded. Again, I heard the tic-tic of the metal. It no longer mattered, I was a proud graduate, one known as a "night crawler." And I had already been approved for Ordination as a Deacon in the United Methodist Church.

The graduates processed out of the sanctuary into the garden of the Church. I had two envelopes. I was proudly taking pictures with family and friends who had attended the graduation, when someone asked what is in the other envelope. In all of the excitement, I had never looked inside of it. I opened the envelope and there was a hand written award certificate, but there was something else. It was a check for $2000. Initially I wondered, was this for the church? No, it was a check with my name on it. I had to go and find Dr. Howard, who was also looking for me. He was a distinguished looking gentleman with a bushy beard and easy to spot. When I found him, I fell into his arms with tears streaming down. He said, Ouida, "this award is given annually to two persons whose ministry brings together the community and the world. And you were the only one in the Internship program that demonstrated that." All I could say was, "thank you." I have always thought of myself as a 'servant minister.' "Be careful not to practice your righteousness in front of others to be seen by them. If you do, you will have no reward from your Father in heaven," Matthew 6:1.

Ministry was all encompassing and I was overjoyed to have been chosen by God to proclaim the word of the Lord. It was my goal to always write a new sermon for each Sunday, one that came from the Lectionary text as I was taught by Rev. Zan. I challenged myself to always be relevant and relational. I did not copy the sermons of others, I just wanted to preach what God put into my heart. And that it what I did in the cities of Sherman and Denison. Community has always been a part of my life and I participated with these cities. Outreach was near and dear to my heart, and I found partnership among the people of the communities.

When the Haven Chapel Church learned of a Shalom Zone, they were willing to get trained. We received the initial conference donation for completion of the training, and we had big goals. Initially, we hosted a Health Fair and Back to School Festival.

The Shalom Team was comprised of members from several of the local churches. As we planned, we were aware that we would need a tent for the main event. Since we wanted to entertain the children, we invited a Puppet Ministry from one of the churches. The school principals from the elementary, middle and high schools were invited to speak to persons who were in attendance. And music was free flowing throughout the day. The children of our community would have to have shots, therefore, we took the old Parsonage next door to the church, cleaned and painted it. The Grayson County Nurses were willing to come on-site to give shots. We planned a huge event, getting the Police Department to close the streets in all four directions so that we could place a basketball goal in the middle of the street for the youth to play. We purchased school supplies

Mrs. Gloria Walker of Haven Chapel UMC understood. She facilitated the donation of property to the church, on which we built a playground and a parking lot. The land was donated to us and we wanted to build a parking lot for the church that could double as a basketball court. Once we owned the land, we were unable to find anyone in the Grayson County area that would pour the concrete. I was a woman Pastor and all of the contractors ignored my call. We eventually hired a contractor from Ft. Worth to come to Denison and pour the concrete. The concrete for the parking lot would not have been possible without the support of the Waples United Methodist Church and the First National Bank of Denison who made significant donations. There is a sense that when one has a purpose to do something special help comes from all directions. I wrote an article for the Sherman Democrat Newspaper about our Shalom Zone Ministry because I believed that it provided tremendous ministry to the Denison community and it became a front page story. Also, the K-TEN television station in Sherman/Denison area called me to do an interview. The work of ministry of a small church with a big vision had shone light on the servants of God. The Shalom Ministry was born out of the crisis in the Watts Area of Los Angeles, CA. It was to bring peace to areas across our United Methodist Church and brought to visibility the community residents and their leadership. And that's what Shalom Ministries did for the Haven Chapel United Methodist Church in Denison, Texas.

It was our goal that the church would be the sponsor, but we recruited residents of the community to participate and even lead the project. The work of this ministry was new to the residents, but we found willing supporters. I recall the night that I spoke with the United Methodist Women of the Waples Church and at the end of the meeting an envelope was handed to me. When I got to the car, I opened the envelope and there were 5 one hundred bills contained therein. This was totally unexpected, but was one of the lessons that I learned in life, "we must walk by faith and not by sight." Those five hundred dollars provided part of the matching funds that we needed to move our project ahead. When I was invited back to speak with the Waples Church during Sunday School, I boldly asked the question, "where are the bankers in this town?" The very next day, I received a call from one of the Banks in town which offered us a challenge grant. I was told that if I could raise $10,000 they would match the funds. I shared my conversation with the church and we began our campaign. I ask each member to give as much as they could and we then approached the community. When one of the local doctors heard our challenge, he asked me how much I needed, but then we had $9500 and he told me to come by his office and pick up the last $500. This project taught me that doing things for God requires courage.

I was a Pastor in two different and distinct cities, but within my heart was to be a servant of all of the people. I had big dreams for ministry, but it takes teams to make things happen. Since I was a full-time Pastor, I had the time to attend meetings and get to know people. I attended a Pastors' meeting that was held monthly at Austin College in Sherman. I was the only Methodist and woman in attendance, therefore, I got to know and make connections with all of the persons who were in attendance. And I want to reiterate the importance of connections. Through my participation with the Austin College Ministerial Alliance, I was able to get the assistance of the students to assist with community projects. When the playground was built on the property on Walker Street in Denison, the students came and help to put the lining in the sandbox. They further did projects with the St. James Church, painting and other odd jobs.

I was intimately involved in the St. James Church since the parsonage was located next door. And with my outward focused ministry, I spent a lot of time with the children of the church, many of whom lived in the Sherman Housing Authority. Each Wednesday evening, I would drive to the Sherman Housing Development to pick up the children in my car and bring them to the church for a meeting. I would cook and serve dinner to the children and would not allow them to wash the dishes. I wanted them to have the opportunity to be children, if only during those hours. We would then enter into a study and further a time of games.

It was not long before word had spread that St. James was having Children/Youth Ministry on Wednesdays. There were so many children desirous of attending that we needed additional transportation to bring them. It was my understanding that we had a Missions Team in the Sherman-Mckinney District and I then made application for grant money from them to purchase transportation. I learned that we needed to have some funds in order to get support. Since I was working for the City of Dallas and living there, my position as a Council Assistant gave me the opportunity of coming into contact with a diverse community. One evening, at the request of my Councilmember, Dr. Charles Tandy, I was to present a key to the city to the Director of the Mississippi Mass Choir who was guest of Rev. Arman Brown, the Director of the DFW Mass Choir. At the time the DFW Mass Choir was very popular in our area and it became my idea to invite them to Sherman to put on a concert.

Though we were a tiny membership Church in Sherman, we had great dreams of growing and doing great ministry in the community. After a discussion with the members of St. James, I placed a call to Rev. Brown. He said they would come, we set the date, made the advertisement material and secured the location. The concert was to be held at Austin College in the Auditorium. I was told that the seating capacity was 959. The agreement with Rev. Brown was for $600 to bring the choir and we printed our own tickets, made posters, sent the announcement to all of the churches of the Sherman-McKinney District where the Rev. Tom Graves was the Superintendent.

The word spread like wild fire, "how was that tiny little church going to fill the auditorium?" But we had great faith and we believed that nothing was impossible with God. The tickets had to be sold for an affordable price. We had to have a local person to be our lead and Phiebie Hutchins was chosen. She was our member and everyone in the city knew her. Our ticket price was set at $5 each and we did a souvenir booklet to highlight the event. And may I tell you that my local ticket sales persons were the members of the St. James Church. Andrea Mckee stood in her front yard on the day of the event and the people were rolling up purchasing 5 tickets at a time. And the District Office was making sales to the churches of our District.

The concert was set to begin at 7 p.m., and at 5 p.m., I received a call at home from one of the members who had arrived early and the people were already arriving in order to get the best seats. I shall never forget that night because there were reserved seating for Pastors and their spouses and everything else was general seating. As I stood before that massive crowd that had filled every inch of that auditorium, I was almost speechless. I offered a welcome and a prayer with great enthusiasm. Our event was a huge success. We paid the Choir and had more than $5,000 left to help us get transportation for our church.

Our church, (I) made a grant request to the District Missions Team. My grant was denied, because the District was aware that ours was a poor church. The statement that came back to me was, "even if we gave you a grant for a bus, you would not be able to afford the insurance on it." It was a grave disappointment, but I learned for this experience, "If God be for you, who can be against." Romans 8:31.

Although we were not granted the funds for the bus, there was a Senior Citizen in our church who was under the Guardianship of her nephew, Ronnie Holland. She had an oil well pumping in Sherman and he was her Custodian. And when he heard our story and the good work that we were doing, he said, "Have the Trustees of the Church to go and look for you a bus." I asked the Trustees to go and look for a bus, but they did not have the time to get around to it. About three months later, he called the Parsonage and left a message, "I have found a bus in Arlington (which was where he lived) I would like for you to come to dealership and check on it. It is reserved in your name." I went the very next day and test drove it. I called him back to say, "I test drove the bus today and it drives like a cream puff." A message on his machine. The very next evening when I arrived home, the machine message, "I have paid for the bus, you may go and pick it up." Without hesitation, I picked up a member of the church and we drove to Arlington and picked up the bus. Our first action was to insure the bus and then get our church name and the Pastor's name printed on the bus.

Our little church was so excited, we instantly began a pickup service for Sunday mornings and Wednesday evening. Our 15 passenger bus on Wednesdays was loaded with about 30 children. Not only did we have dinner, a lesson, but we were able to take them to the other side of town where there was a real park with walking tracks, ball diamonds and a swimming pool. And what joy it was to see the kids roam freely and enjoy themselves. The bus Ministry became known throughout the city for our outreach to community. We were written up in the local newspaper for our outreach to impoverished children and youth. A local company came to teach our children etiquette. She cooked a meal, brought her own dishes, silverware, and glassware. She taught the children how to use their silverware and they were so sweet. We told our story to the local newspaper. We were then invited to bring 10 of our children to dinner when the Chamber of Commerce invited an African American businessman to Austin College for dinner. We were not allowed to sit together, rather two Youth were placed at each table. One of the best compliments for me on that evening was when one of the boys who had attended the class rushed over to me and asked, "Rev. Lee which fork am I to use for the salad?"

We now had transportation and could travel, therefore we were invited to the Waples United Methodist Church for a dinner highlighting Youth. But the day that I received a call from the Tanglewood Resort Retreat Center inviting me to bring all of our children and Youth for a special Day Camp was unbelievable. They would bring their vans and we were to be prepared to stay all day. The buses arrived at the church and drove us to Tanglewood. Each child was given a Tanglewood t-shirt and our first stop was fishing. Tanglewood provided the camp leaders and they allowed all of the children to catch a fish, for many their first. We then loaded onto a boat and were taken out on the water in true cruise fashion where lunch was provided. We docked and the camp Counselors came out on wave runners and took the kids for a ride. Even now as I remember that day, my eyes become misty. We never knew who paid for all of this, but it was a day etched in the memory of every child.

Haven Chapel had celebrated their heyday when we did the community event, and so had St. James with the big concert. What were we to do next? Ministry afforded me the opportunity to visit so many of the church where I encountered persons who owned their own small businesses. It was time for the community to know about all of this. After assembling a Team of Visionaries, I shared my idea of showcasing the local businesses. We already knew that the communities loved music. As we began to toss together ideas, we began to vision bringing together people from the surrounding communities. There were Black Leaders all around us, therefore, we planned the very first Texomaland Black Expo which was held in the Sid Richardson Auditorium of Sherman. The outpouring was more than 700 people and our featured guest speaker was the Honorable John Wiley Price of Dallas. Vendors from the Tri-Counties of Grayson, Cooke and Colin were all involved. The event also hosted a Male Fashion Show and the Federated Choirs of Sherman sang at the event. Mayor in Whitewright at the time was Bill Goodson. I was introduced to him by his sister who lived in Dallas, TX. We became fast friends and along with his wife, we focused on how we could be engaged in making the world a better place. Stepping out in faith makes the world a different place and offers many exciting opportunities.

While I continued my work as a Pastor in the North Texas Conference, I was invited to become a member of the Conference Council on Ministries. It was there that I met, Mary Brooke Casad whom I later learned was the daughter of a Bishop. She had great ideas and visions for our Conference and I was excited to be part of the team. The Bishop at the time was William "Bill" Oden and it was his vision to connect the NTC with the Russian Conference. One evening as we sat around giving reports, the Global Missions Team recommended that they would take a trip to Prague. My question, "what person of color will be part of that team?" No response was given that night, but early the next week, I received a call from Mary Brooke who asked, "Would you like to go with us to Prague?"

My quick and easy response was, "Yes." I already had a passport from an earlier cruise to the Bahamas.

This was the trip of a lifetime. I scrambled to gather my funds, because I did not intend to be a burden to the Conference. As we board the big jet liner, I had more than $1100 in my money belt. Little did I know that I would bring most of it back home. The Conference paid all expenses. We ate family style and the bill was paid by our leader, Mary Brooke. We arrived in Prague and shared the accommodations of one of the Methodist Churches. The transportation drove across the curb and the wall separated in order to let us drive in back of the church. Our rooms were hotel style. Bishop and Marilyn met us there the next morning, they were on a worldwide tour.

I could not believe the expanse of Prague. We stood on one of the three bridges and took pictures. Can you imagine the eyes of this young woman who had grown up in the piney woods of East Texas and was now walking on one of the three Bridges of Prague, walking through their mansions and shopping for garnets in one of the many jewelry stores? It was a journey that began to open the door to the many adventurous places on God's beautiful earth would allow me to see.

We visited many churches in Prague and heard the many stories regarding the ultimate effect that Communism had on them. We were told that the churches most often were the places that the KGB, translated in English as the "Committee for State Security" from 1954 to 1991. As we visited several of the churches, we saw evidence of their presence through the wires that were still hanging from the ceilings. Communism had taken a huge toll on the Christian Churches because they had to go underground in order to meet. It was unbelievable for me to see the huge Cathedrals on the streets, but when we gathered with the church at a campsite a few days later, we met the few who were attempting to renew the church. We could not communicate, except with an interpreter. This was a different place in the world. The cars were extremely small and whenever the drivers would park, the ignitions were taken out of the car and put in their pockets in order to assure that when we were ready to depart, the car would still be there.

After a few days in the city of Prague, we were taken out to the countryside. And though the city of Prague was filled with people, and everyone had a cell phone, we were now going to the country. We drove for miles down deserted highways. One would observe nuclear reactors in the distance as we drove along. My companion in the car was Rev. Gary Mueller (now Bishop Mueller of the Arkansas Conference) and we sat quietly in this tiny car surrounded by our large luggage. It was deep within the country among trees so tall they appeared to be touching the heavens. On several occasions, we observed people laying along the road in the tall grass.

When we finally arrived at the camp, we met with others who were representing various churches from the Russian diaspora. The three single (without companions) women in our group were shown to our accommodations. Three beds in a room above the cafeteria. When we gathered for meals, there were no plates, only a piece of silverware. Breads were placed in the middle of the table and we would line up to be served our meals from a common pot with bowls in our hands. Though it did not look good, it was tasty and I was ravenously hungry. We worshipped together later that night and sang songs that I could only hum. I knew the words of at least one, but on the pages "Amazing Grace" had no familiarity.

The next leg of the journey was to visit the various churches. Can you imagine the shock for me when we went to live with families, and I shared with a young German speaking woman, accompanied by the interpreter? When we arrived at the church, the entrance door to the sanctuary open at the sidewalk and we drove into the backyard through the lobby of the church. In back there was a beautiful house on the second floor. When it was time for bed, she said, you can sleep in my bed. It was a pallet on the floor in the corner of the room. I was in shock, but I was wise enough to be grateful. The other startling thing was they had the best breads, but it was served mostly with cheese. Life in my infancy had trained me well, we did not have meat at every meal. And the countryside held many similarities – extremely tall trees and dark nights.

After several days at the Campsite, we were taken back to Prague for one last night. Early the next morning, we were advised that we would be taking the train to Zurich, Switzerland. Our expert traveler prepared us for the journey. Mary Brooke advised us that we would make many stops and that everything was timed. We would have to get our luggage and get from one train to the other expeditiously, or we might miss our connection. My luggage was huge and now I had picked up a glass bowl which I purchased in Prague that had to make it home. Our group always attempted to sit together and during one of those times, Mary Brooke said to me, "I am in culture shock, nobody speaks our language." My response, "I have not seen a black person in two weeks and when I finally saw one on the train, she spoke another language." Wow, what a journey.

We traveled the countryside on the train and the scenery was absolutely beautiful. The train ride was so smooth that it felt as if we were riding in a Cadillac. For the most part, the tracks were high and our view from the windows reveal green valleys and occasional churches. We arrived in Zurich on a Saturday evening and checked into a hotel. We were told that the city basically closed at 6 p.m., therefore, we made a quick trip out to dinner. The next morning, we boarded a train again for a short distance out to the Swiss Alps. Transportation up to the Alps was by van. Our lodging there was Hotel Victoria, which at that time was owned by the Methodist Church. This time, I was given a private room which faced the mountains. Outside, I had a clear view of a waterfall that flowed. The town that we were near was Meiringer, Switzerland. The only way for us to get to the town was by a gondola and each one held a maximum of 50 passengers. One day during our visit in the Alps, we took gondolas that held a maximum of 4 passengers. Riding over the tops of trees was not my favorite mode of transportation, however, if we were to see the Alps up close and personal, we had to ride them. We would get to a certain level and stop, wait for transportation to the next level. The second level was high enough for me, because the next level appeared to be in the clouds.

At Hotel Victoria, we met with the Bishop of Russia to visit about the business of ministry with the North Texas Conference. The churches that I served were much too small to make connection, but I was there in a surreal way, listening, taking notes and visioning for how I could do ministry. We did not go back to Prague to make our flight back to the United States, we flew direct from Zurich to Dallas Fort Worth on Zurich Airlines. On the day before our return trip we left Hotel Victoria and journeyed by van back to train depot. It was there that I saw and was able to communicate with an African. He was extremely tall and spoke the Kings' English with a British accent. Little did I know that God was preparing me for International Travel.

Once back in the United States, with full-time ministry as my focus, the St. James/Haven Chapel Charge became the center of my learning and growing in ministry. Ministry was not without its' challenges. The Haven Chapel Church was asked to take an ad in one of the Baptist Churches in the community. We did not have much money, but we wanted to be supportive, therefore we sent a check to pay for the ad. The next Sunday morning, I came in to find an envelope addressed to Sister Ouida Lee with our check in it say, "We believe in doing things Gods' way, therefore we are returning your check."

Another incidence that is still on mind today is a Baptist Church in Sherman invited me to an event and when I arrived, I went to the Pastor's Office, leaving my granddaughter in the sanctuary. When I said to the Pastor, "I received an invitation from your church to attend this program." He stood up and told the other Pastors, "let me handle this." He came to the door and step so close to me that I had to back up, and remarked, "If you are here for a program, you can go out and take a seat on the front row." I extended my hand to him and said, "thank you, I will not be staying." I walked out, grabbed my grand child's hand and she asked, "Where are we going?" I said, "We are not welcomed here, and we are leaving." When I got to my car, I raised my foot and dusted my shoes, as I got into the car. For the bible teaches in Matthew 10:14, "If anyone will not welcome you or listen to your words, leave that home or town and shake the dust off your feet."

I was invited back, several weeks later, because an AFLCIO Union man who heard of my plight. He insisted that I was part of the welcomed community because my church was a member of the City-wide Ushers group. They wanted to take a picture, in that same church and I was seated in the center. The picture was to depict the Pastors of the City Wide Ushers of Sherman. St. James United Methodist Church was part of that group and I would be included, even if the Pastor wanted to shut me out, or place me in an inferior position.

I am so thankful for the Federated Ushers of Sherman and the Federated Choirs of Sherman, because they provided huge support to our congregation during times of financial struggles. The Ushers met on the third Sunday of each month and one of the Pastors of the Affiliated Churches would preach and all of the Ushers would attend and share an offering. The Pastor was given a token of appreciation and the Congregation where the worship service was held kept the additional finances for their churches. Likewise, with the Federated Choirs, on the Second Sunday of each month the Choirs would visit one of the Churches and the offering was left with the Church that was the host. Approximately, three times each year, each of the groups would visit the affiliated churches. These were joyous times of celebration for our churches, we supported each other and had great fellowship. As the only female Pastor of the congregations, the people were very welcoming to me.

It was the year 1996 that I began my full-time journey in the Sherman Denison communities. Although I had been serving as a Student Local Pastor in the North Texas Conference as a To Be Supplied (TBS) position, I was now authorized. Pastors in the United Methodist Church are required to earn a Masters' of Divinity Degree in order to be Ordained. I met those qualifications in May 1996 and was Ordained as a Deacon (a two-step process in 1996, first a Deacon and two years later an Elder). The Masters' Degree alone does not qualify the Candidate Minister, there are stringent interview requirements.

On the day of my interview, I sat before 24 persons at a table who threw questions at me from all directions. Interviews never really bother me, because if I feel qualified for a particular position, it is difficult to shake me. But this was different. Although I had passed the interview, the question was, "Are you willing to leave your full-time position with City Government?" It was my personal goal to go to work for the church in a part-time status and continue working full-time. They told me that was impossible. I made a decision that would affect me and my family for some time. For you see, full-time Pastors had to live on the property where they were appointed, and that was 75 miles from my home. However, this was what I had devoted my life to for the past 5 years. But it would also affect my home life. Our youngest child had graduated high school and was in College at Grambling State University. Though there were no children at home, my husband was adamant about the fact that he would not be living in Sherman. And now there is Ordination before me, "Would my husband be my escort for the service?" Reluctantly, he agreed to come with me for the practice for the service and escorted me into the worship at the First United Methodist Church in downtown Dallas.

This was such an emotional time for me, torn between being the wife my husband had expected, not a preacher and the challenges that I had faced all along the journey. And I should add, all of the insult that I had endured as a servant leader, attempting to follow my calling. When Bishop Bruce called me forward, it was as if I was all alone that night. My tears began to flow and were unstoppable. When the Ordinands were asked to face the sanctuary and the Bishop came to share my hands, I was crying so uncontrollably that he gave me two hugs. I had been authenticated by the United Methodist Church to "take thine authority." Wow, after 5 years in seminary, countless hours of study, people who walked away from me…"take thine authority."

I was so thankful that in June I was Ordained and appointed to do full-time ministry. This was the beginning of a brand new journey. I resigned from the City of Dallas on the same day I had begun my employment 25 years earlier. It was the middle of the week and the pay period, but I did not want to stay one day past the 25 years.

I received a Proclamation signed by the Honorable Mayor Ron Kirk and a plaque from my fellow employees. There was also a memento presented to me by my immediate supervisor which has held a prominent place everywhere I have lived and it read, "See, I am sending an angel ahead of you to guard you along the way and to bring you to the place I have prepared," Exodus 23:20. I was 47 years old and had I been willing to wait just 3 more years, I could have begun receiving my retirement income. I must say that I made so many foolish choices in my life, but in retrospect, I believe that the Lord was leading me and ordering my footsteps, and that an angel was going ahead of me. And even more, I had a mind made up to give my best in service and through compassionate love to all whom I would encounter.

I moved to the church parsonage in Sherman the next week. It was quiet and the house was tiny and kind of unstable, two bedrooms, a living room, kitchen and study in the back. But I was Rev. Ouida Lee

Appointed as the Senior Pastor of the St. James/Haven Chapel Charge. The members told Bishop Blake that if they were ever going to grow, they believed that I would be the one who could do it. Bishop Blake questioned me, "Do you want to stay here as their Pastor?" I responded, if they wanted me to be there with them, I was willing to serve there. Throughout the years that I was appointed there, they had all supported me, and that was important to me.

The Charge could not afford full-time support for me: therefore, there would have to be funding for my support. One day shortly after I arrived for work at the Haven Chapel Church, Rev. Dr. Leighten Farrell, Senior Pastor of the Highland Park United Methodist Church of Dallas came to visit me, along with my Superintendent, Dr. Thomas Graves. He wanted to hear my vision, if the Highland Park Church was going to support my salary. I shared how I wanted to see our church grow and be community involved through outreach ministries. I further shared that I wanted to get our church on the local Cable Television show. I don't know how convinced he was with my vision, but HPUMC funded the grant.

As a person who was accustomed to having a full-time position, I made my way to the church every day. When I would arrive, there were men standing on the corner of the building. Courageously, I would ask them why they were standing on the corner of our church, and where they attended church. The next morning they would be back again, I asked what their Pastor's name and does he know that you are over here standing on the corner of our church. They would move down the block. They were dealing drugs and fearlessly, I believed that God would protect me. I had already found children in both churches and though I could not get their parents to attend Prayer on Tuesdays at Haven Chapel, they came. We would sing songs that I taught them from the hymn books and I would pray.

One of the challenges that faced both of these churches annually was Apportionment. We did not have the money, so we taxed ourselves by asking each adult member of the congregation to give $100 for the Church Anniversaries and that money would be used to pay the annual assessment, sometimes with a few dollars to spare. These were big days for the congregation, we would invite a local Pastor and church to preach for the afternoon services. And dinner would be served to all who attended.

Our churches were known for doing special fundraisers. Mrs. Viola Walker shared with us the idea of doing a "bean dinner" in downtown Denison. The first year, we raised more than $600 selling beans and cornbread, no meat. The next year, another church stole our idea. So we decided to do a Banquet and host it at the Country Club and invited Bishop

William Oden to be our speaker. He would not accept an honorarium. The next year we hosted a banquet and invited County Commissioner John Wiley Price to be our speaker. He came as our guest, but when we offered to pay him, he signed the check and gave it back to us. Of course we hosted Women's Day and a Women's Conference. Big things can be done in small communities, if one has the faith to step forward. I am so appreciative of the support that I received from the Women of the Haven Chapel Church and their willingness to walk alongside of me.

St. James was not treated any differently. We hosted special Mother's Day Celebrations, taking pictures of the mothers and their families. And in order to pay our Apportionments there we asked the same $100 per adult member, but we also did Patrons' list in order that each person could afford to pay the $100. We did a Debutante for Christ Pageant at the church and raised more than $4500. The funds from these events help to pay our bills. And we loved Revivals, where I would invite my Clergy sisters to come and preach for us. We hosted a Mission and Brotherhood program for the community and one of the Pastors came out of the Brotherhood meeting where a male Pastor was bashing me during the class. He was the friend of one of the women of the congregation who had been attending our church and in the class, he said to a Methodist Preacher, Rev. Jack Castle, "Women are supposed to keep silent in the church." Pastor Castle was offended and very angry. He told me, "Get rid of that guy, out of your church." Wow!

Easter was a very special time for the Sherman Community, we hosted the Ministerial Alliance during Holy Week. The President stood in our pulpit and said, "We want to thank Sister Lee for hosting us this year.'" When it came time for me to make remarks, I said, "We are honored to host the Ministerial Alliance. But when I was a little girl, back in Henderson, TX when we would go to the courthouse to use the restroom, my mother always went to the Colored Girls' restroom. I used to wonder when she was going to grow up and go to the Women's restroom. And now I am wondering when I am going to grow up. Here I am the Pastor of this church and I am still being called Sister Lee." A hush went over the house. There were some things that I could not allow to pass. I was a dues paying member of that Alliance.

Now I must tell you that one of the young preachers in the crowd night came to my office and said, "You should not be surprised by that remark, after all, that is what the Bible says." My response, "Do you know whose office you are in right now? You are in my office and I am asking you to leave right now." Make no mistake, I was aware of what Paul said in I Corinthians 14:34 "Women should remain silent in the churches." But I also read Paul's words to the Romans chapter 16 verse 2-3, "I commend to you our sister Phoebe, a deacon of the church in Cenchreae. I ask you to receive her in the Lord in a way worthy of his people and to give her any help she may need from you, for she has been the benefactor of many people, including me." (NIV). Perhaps it was growth that led Paul to speak these words, but from these words, we find that he is a supporter of women in Ministry. Study!

During my years in Sherman, I totally immersed myself in ministry. And since my income had dropped significantly, I decided to get myself a part-time job. I was hired by the Grayson County Health Department to educate women in the community regarding Breast Cancer. It was my assignment to meet women in the community, through the churches and set up meetings to a show video and allow the women to examine a cancerous breast. This was ideal for me, I loved people and it allowed me to get to know them in more personal ways. During a meeting in which I explained my role in the Health Department, I was approached by a member of the Cable One staff members. As we departed the doors, she said to me, "You have the nicest voice. Would you be interested in doing a television show?"

"A television show? Me?" My immediate response was "Yes.". She handed me her business card and said, "Call me." I did so as soon as I got back to the church. This was an answer to my prayer to have our church on TV.

Cable One was a local cable station in Sherman and she was interested in me doing a talk show. I told her that I would be honored to do so. She asked that I get a male companion to co-host. I called another Pastor and invited him to share with me. He agreed to participate, but after the first show aired, he would not respond to my calls. When I called the station to tell them what had happened, I was told to do the show alone. The content was whatever I selected. The show was called, "Talk of the Town." It was my decision to invite every African American leader in the community to our show. The station provided the production staff and I would invite the guests. Every African American Club, Fraternal Order and Sisterhood was invited. I would make announcements about the upcoming events. And as a leader in the community, serving on the Auxiliary of the Wilson and Jones Hospital, new doctors in town were invited new businesses in town, including restaurants.

The highlight and most highly watched program was when I realized that Sherman and Denison were in competition with each other. Annually, there was the "Bury the Hatchet" football game. And it was my vision to invite the Principals of Sherman and Denison Schools, along with the Presidents of the Student Bodies. Each Principal was invited to share the highlights of their schools, along with the Presidents. Their closing remarks were regarding who would win and get to bury the Hatchet. When I walked into the station on the day following the airing of that show, the Station Manager called me into his office and shared the stats. As a result of that I was invited to participate on the early morning show on K-TEN TV in Denison. The question that came to me from the interviewer was, "How did you come up with the idea of a Talk Show and bringing together the competitive schools." As a community involved person, I had my hand on the pulse beat of the community. And I listened. Talk of the Town aired every week for one hour. I was told by one classroom teacher that since I was the only Black program in the area, she would sometimes view my shows in her classroom.

My role as Pastor in a community with full time to do ministry in small churches led me to many diverse places: the home of Dr. Bueker, a professor at Austin College, Wilson Jones Hospital as a member of Auxiliary, The Aids Resource Center of Texoma as a Board Member, Member of the NAACP of Sherman, The Texoma Area Agency on Aging, The Texoma Business and Professional Women's Club, A Mentor for the Juvenile Justice Program, and a member of both the Sherman Ministerial Alliance and the Ministers' Alliance of Sherman. Our congregations were financially deprived, but the richness of engagement with the community made my time in service rich.

The Great Days of Service is where I encountered working with the Mayor of Sherman. He was a great leader and member of the First United Methodist Church of Sherman. Each year during the Great Days of Service, we visited Nursing Homes, the jail and we scraped and painted houses around the city. On one eventful nights that we were in jail teaching a bible lesson, a storm turned off the power in the jail. Everything went pitch black. We were advised to sit still because they were working on the problem. May I tell you that was a frightening night? However, it was not long before the emergency light came on. During the interim, we sat locked in the jail in total darkness.

Since the community had enriched my life in so many ways, during the year of 1998, I decided to host a Christmas Party for my community partners. I extended the invitation and cooked for the more than 50 people whom I invited. Approximately 35 showed up, and we feasted royally. The very next day, I received a call from Bill and Joan Douglass, the owners of Douglass Distributing Company. I knew them because they were members of the Grace United Methodist Church in the city of Sherman. Joan asked me to meet her at her home that day around noon. When I arrived, she shared, "Bill and I were so impressed with what you did on last night, and we would like to give you $500 so that you may be a blessing to your community. And we would like to give you $500 for spending it for us." I started to talking, and Joan interrupted, "Did you hear what I said?" Yes. I had heard her, but I was stunned, what did I do to deserve this? "Yes, I would be honored to do this for you all." But she added, "You must not tell anyone where the money came from." Ideas began to spin in my head, I would spend the money on the children that I picked up on Wednesday night from the Housing Projects. She gave me $1000 in two checks. Wow!!

It was close to Christmas, but I believe that I had enough time to get the sizes of every child, and I did so. I went to the home of the children and got the sizes for each of them. I shopped, Kmart, J C Penney until each child had a set clothes. I got boxes and wrapped them and delivered them to their homes the weekend of Christmas. Each child came to church dressed in their clothes and they were so proud. I prepared fruit baskets for the senior adults in the church. It was Christmas cheer for all. I had some money left for myself, but I was more interested in making each of them happy. I am reminded, "Give and it will be given to you, full measure, pressed down, shaken together and running over," Luke 6:38.

On Sunday morning, all of the children were dressed in the attire that I had meticulously shopped for each of them. And the senior adults, that I bought fruit and put together baskets, were enjoyed by each of them.

I believe that we are blessed to be a blessing. It was such a joy to see the smiles on the faces of children who otherwise might not have gotten new attire for the holidays.

Though the churches were small in membership, they were big in love. And there were members who joined us along the way. And I learned that if one is in ministry to make a difference, there are many opportunities in the small town, and when you genuinely care for other people, they will care

about you. The Herald Democrat newspaper embraced the stories that I wrote to them, a couple even made front page news. Every week, I would share with the advertising section the topic and the text from which I would be preaching. And we never failed to let them know when we had special guests coming to share in our worship. One of the things that I brought with me was my love and compassion for people. I would visit the members in their homes, the hospitals and nursing homes. I would always offer prayer and sometimes I sang songs to them. And if there was a death in the family, I would be there to console and preach a sermon that embraced the life of the deceased. And if a member lost a loved one, no distance was too far to accompany them. Those actions were the beginning of a tradition that would follow me throughout my journey in ministry.

One of the ways that I managed the Charge was to keep each one posted on what the other was doing. And I did that through a monthly newsletter. One column was devoted to the St. James Church and the other to Haven Chapel. I would share the number of persons in attendance during the month, the number of new members and the events that were taking place along with the plans that were being made in each church. It served as a motivator for the sister congregation. The Superintendent at the time was Dr. Jim Pledger and he shared with me one day that he had always had trouble with Pastors for the Charge because one congregation loved the Pastor, while the other complained. But he asked me what I was doing because both of the congregations loved me. My response was I attempt to treat them both the same. They were different, one was highly educated and the other had limited education. One was more financially stable, the other would attempt to do their very best. One was a youthful congregation, the other more elderly. But my belief is that if genuine love is extended to each congregation and the members know that you are not spending more time with one than the other, you constantly share that you believe in them, and you share each of their successes, they will live up to the difference.

The Children really made a difference in the life of the St. James Church. Mrs. Pauline Harley Neblett, shared with me that Mrs. Malinda Gabriel had great grandchildren who lived near the church. When I found out where they lived, I visited their home and invited them to come to church. When they started attending, I baptized each of them, and the oldest child, Wash McKee was a preteen and he had friends. He took real pride in the fact that he was a new Christian and he must have told all of his friends and several of them came and joined the church and were also Baptized. I was not supposed to be working because I was appointed as a full-time Pastor. However, the money that I was being paid was quite limited. Therefore, I applied for and was accepted as an employee of the Sherman Development Center.

I needed the income to meet my financial obligations. And I wanted to remain committed to my full-time work at the church, so I took the evening shift at the Center. My dear colleague in Ministry, Rev. Nannette Davis (deceased) was really worried for me, because she knew that if the District learned about my employment, I would be held back. She would call me and remind me of the days that we would need to go for our meetings and would often drive me there. She would call and check on me constantly and ask what she could do to help me. The pay was low and the work was unbelievable. I was performing menial tasks, changing patients, helping to bathe and making beds to assure that patients who needed my care were never omitted. One night Nan called and said that she was really concerned because it was really close to the time that we would go before the Board. I agreed to submit my resignation. I wrote the letter and pushed it underneath a locked door. It had only gone under the door that I began to regret my decision. But it was done, I had resigned.

Male support in the churches was limited to older gentlemen who were in their late 70's and the younger men were not committed, so one of the Lay women and I cut the hedges. Not sure what they are called, but they had grown much too tall and they were the sticky ones. We cut them, but when we finished it was too late to pick them up. We would get them the next day. Early the next morning, as I rushed from the house for a meeting, Mrs. Linda Graves was on her knees picking up the debris. When

I opened the back screen door, something fell on the ground. I got a stick and pulled it out and got in the car. I could see Linda, I stopped hastily and she sent on my journey with these words, "Go on to your meeting, I will take care of these." She had gloves and bags and someone who was going to come and pick them up. What manner of woman is this? She was the Superintendent's wife, a dedicated servant of the Most High God. I learned from her the attitude of a servant who expects her blessings to come from God alone. As I got back in the car to rush to the meeting that I was attending, I picked up the envelope. When I opened the Valentine card a check fell out. It was a check for $1000.00, from my dear friend Nan. The card read, this is not a loan. When you can afford to, pass it on. I burst out in tears so pervasively that I had to pull to the side of the road so I could see how to continue to drive. Wow!

During the year 1998, I was interviewed by the Sherman McKinney District Board of Ministry and recommended to the Conference Board of Ordained Ministry for Ordination as Elder of the Church. And when I was interviewed, I was told that my paperwork was a bit weak, but I passed in flying colors. When all of us in our class met together, we learned that my friend who had cheered for and supported me did not pass the Board. We were all so sad and encouraged her to come back the next year. She did and she was ordained.

I received a call from my Clergy Sister Rev. Denise Sawyer who had now relocated back to Nassau, Bahamas after graduating Perkins School of Theology. She asked me to send one of my recorded sermons because they were looking for a preacher to conduct a Revival on the Island. I followed up by sending several cassettes and was extended an invitation to conduct a Revival in Nassau. When I arrived in the country, posters with my picture were posted around the city on restaurant doors, I was shocked. It was a three day Revival and was well attended by the members of the congregation and their guests. It was an amazing experience and each evening, the Prayer Ministry prayed in the rear of the church while I preached.

The two churches would meet together for annual charge conference. And though our ministry was going well, our money often fell short in the St. James Church. Our new District Superintendent was Dr. Thomas Graves and his wife Linda were members in attendance at the First Church of Sherman. However, Linda who was justice focused, was keenly aware of the work that we were doing at St. James. She would occasionally attend our Youth meetings on Wednesdays, and sometimes provide a meal for our group. And it was not above her to come and help us pick up debris around the premises. At our annual Charge Conference, she learned of the small amount of offerings that we received at the St. James Church and the next week, she joined our St. James Church, as an at-large member. From that time throughout my tenure, Linda would contribute $650 per month to our finances.

During my seven years there, we had great ministry and the churches grew to more than 60 plus members at Haven Chapel and 70 plus at the St. James Church. I never requested a move, though the work was challenging, and the money was limited, ministry to the people of God meant more to me. And, I believed that I was doing groundbreaking work as a female Pastor in a conservative, male dominated culture.

I was invited by State Representative Ron Clark, of Grayson County, to open the State House of Representative on March 1, 1999. It was such an honor and I wanted to share the occasion with my granddaughter, Shanel and Nasha McKee, one of the young teens at St. James. We traveled to Austin on Sunday and drove over to the Capitol on Monday. I shared the invocation and we took pictures with Representative Clark. Upon my departure from Sherman in August 2000, I was presented the flag that flew over the Capitol the day that I prayed.

As a member of the African American Ministerial Alliance, which was dominated by Baptist Pastors, I joined because I was member of the Clergy of the City. One of the programs that we supported was the high school graduating classes. And when I learned that we only gave them $25, I suggested that we could do better. It took being a member several years before they would allow me to put forth the idea. I wanted to give each graduate $500, and there was a supportive idea. Each Pastor was asked to recommend 2 women from their churches who would help form a team. We would sell tickets for $25 each, and the Holiday Inn would only charge $10 per meal, allowing us to clear $15 per ticket. The women came together, we had the tickets printed and distributed them to each woman. The event was a complete sell out. The crowd arrived dressed in evening attire and the atmosphere was ecstatic. We presented $500 scholarships to five students and the Ministers Alliance became true leaders of the community. From $25 to $500, that is a 500% increase. "For nothing is impossible with God," Luke 1:37.

At the end of year seven, an Anniversary was planned for me by the St. James Church. Phiebie Hutchins was the chair of the Program Committee. Most of my colleagues from the Alliance were in attendance and it was a program of great celebration. The congregation had grown and there were children and youth totally involved in the church. The women of the Alliance Churches were in attendance, they were so supportive. The Federated Choirs of Sherman and the Federation of Ushers were there, along with all of my male colleagues and their spouses. And most of all my family was there, Mother, Mrs. Pearlie B. Isaac and my sister, Evangelist Sheila Isaac, Mother's consummate driver. I shall always remember the words of my Sister, "Sis, your work is finished here, it is time for you to move on." What did she mean, I loved being here and the community had begun to feel extremely comfortable. Time to move on, I had my own Television Broadcast. "Move on??"

Within weeks, I received a call from my Dr. Tom Graves, District Superintendent, "Ouida, we believe that it is time for you to move back to the Dallas Area." Wow. Move on was real. I was to be appointed to the Hamilton Park United Methodist Church as Associate Pastor. This was a huge move for me. I had always had to pay my Social Security and other taxes out of my limited income, and now the church was paying. When I received my first check, I could not believe the amount, but even more important was my opportunity to serve in a support role and not have all of the responsibilities for raising the budget, planning the programs, advertising and generally executing. There was support staff and new opportunities. I would be working with the Rev. Dr. Ronald Henderson.

In August of 2000, my journey of Ministry began at the Hamilton Park UMC. There was no job description. I was to be support to the Senior Pastor. The Pastor shared that I had been in a demanding position for many years and suggested that I should take an educational trip. I chose to go to Denver, CO to get certified to be a leader of the Disciple Bible Study. The Church would pay for the trip. Wow. In my previous appointment, there were no travel funds, no support staff, no trips that I did not pay for.

My reception at the Hamilton Park was exceptional. When I arrived there were flowers in my office from the men of the church, and the women brought me a basket that was specially prepared for me by a dear friend, the late Charlotte Brewster. A lovely reception was prepared following worship. The women of the church were dynamic and very talented. It was there that I met Mrs. Cheryl Haynes who was heading up the Women's Ministry. I shared with her that there was a ministry for women in the General Church called the Status and Role of Women. She researched it and decided along with her Team that is what their ministry would be called. In such a large church setting, it came to our attention the women did not hold any prominent positions. Our first order of business was to strengthen the women's' leadership within the church. We did a study with the women and we planned our first Annual Women's Conference. When we sought a location, we drove to the Sherman area and viewed the Methodist Campsite and then Tanglewood. Tanglewood was chosen. Plans were made and our first conference had more than 85 women of all ages in attendance.

The Conference was to convene over the weekend and we would worship at the Tanglewood Conference center. The morning worship offering was more than $9000. I had no idea what the funds would be, but the women gave their best and when we turned the offering over to the Church, they told us that we could go again anytime. The Conference was both inspirational and spiritually fulfilling. The Status and Role of Women (SROW) Conference has been ongoing for more than 15 years now, and now women are providing leadership throughout the church.

It was during my first year at Hamilton Park that I received a call that our son, John C. Lee, III who was a student at Grambling State University was being taken to the mental hospital in Shreveport, LA. This was a painful call and the beginning of a painful journey. When I arrived in Shreveport the next day, my son was locked within a secure location. He had no clothes and his shirt was being worn inside out. After a conversation with the staff, I was told that he had been diagnosed as Bipolar Disorder. Further, it could have been a one-time occurrence, or it could be a lifetime illness. I would stay in Louisiana until he was released. He was my baby. And I stayed 5 days, and to further complicate the travel, the city was hit with an ice storm, and my hotel lost it electricity. The highways were clear to the hospital, but the tree limbs were covered with thick ice. In my room, I went to sleep each night in total darkness, although that may have been indicative of this difficult time in my life. I visited my son each day and prayed for his healing. On the morning of the sixth day, they released him to come home with me. He was medicated heavily, and slept most of the way. I was glad because I did not know what to expect from his actions. I had just begun my new position at HPUMC and when I returned the Treasurer asked me if I had bills for my hotel. Of course I did, she said, "I should have already ordered you a charge card, so bring the bill to me when you receive it." I did and she paid it.

This was not a one-time occurrence; it was the beginning of a new journey that heavily involved me. As soon as we arrived home, he began to feel better and said he was ready to return to school. He had his medication and knew how he was to take it, but he was unwilling to take the medicine, which would spun him into new episodes. My husband and I allowed him to return to school after a few weeks. He had always ridden the bus to school during the time I was in Sherman, but when he came home for the summer, I purchased him a car.

The Hamilton Park Church was very receptive to my preaching style and I spent time getting to know the members of the congregation. Since we had two services each Sunday, I would go and have breakfast, or at least sit with the earlier crowd after worship. I had a very collegial relationship with all of the members of the congregation. We also began a Wednesday night worship in the Chapel and gave the opportunity for some of the other women and men who felt called to share their witness with the congregation. The service was well received and attended by the congregants.

Many of the Friday evenings, I would be alone at the church and would be invited by the Intercessory Prayer Ministry to join them in Prayer. I believed that I knew how to pray, but this ministry challenged me because they were so committed and had such great faith in the things that they prayed about. It would have been easy for me to pretend that I was too busy to join them in prayer, because I often would be working on my sermons. However, I was intrigued at how they stood so firmly on the word of God in their prayers. As I drew closer to them, and joined them on both Friday evenings and Monday mornings, I began to grow in the understanding that God's word was even more powerful than I had believed. We prayed about everything. And we would sit together and hear the testimonies of the move of God in our lives. This was a time of deep spiritual growth for me personally and little did I know that my life was being anchored in prayer and faith for a future that I did not know that I would experience.

It was during my first year at Hamilton Park that I began my role with the Perkins School of Theology mentoring young men and women in ministry through the Internship Office. My first student was a student whose role was to serve a community ministry in the West Dallas area. Throughout my time of serving with the Intern Office, I assisted 6 students through the process. Several of those students served at the Church where I was Pastor.

It had always been my goal to pursue the Doctorate of Ministry Degree, and I believed that now was the time. I shared with the Dr. Henderson my goal and he suggested that I give myself a year on the staff before I began. I accepted his suggestion. And in the fall of 2001, I began my pursuit of the Doctorate of Ministry with a focus on Urban Ministry. I was intrigued by this topic because I could sit in my office and see the drug dealers on the corner across the street from the church. The Hamilton Park Community would be my area of study, and there was Mrs. Sadie Gee, a faithful Lay Woman, who would tell me the whole story of the beginning of this community. She owned the deed to the first lot that was sold in the Hamilton Park Community. The doctoral project was going to center on the church being the center of the communal life of the community and from its needs would evolve the ministry plan of the church.

Another part of the work that I would be doing for the church was to write a devotional each week for the newsletter. I had learned from the Rev. Dr. Zan Holmes that there is much in the Psalms and that to unearth the truth from them was no easy work. Therefore, each week, based on the Lectionary text, I wrote a brief devotion. The devotions became my first book, *"A Sip from the Well,"* which I self-published prior to my departure from Hamilton Park.

The year 2001 I began my doctoral studies. Throughout my life, I had never had the pleasure of attending school as a full-time student, but being appointed in Dallas and not having another job afforded me the opportunity to do so. This was a very exciting season for me, because I was thoroughly engaged in ministry, and as the Rev. Dr. Michael W. Walker had shared with me, before I announced my call, "Prepare yourself to be a leader and not to simply do a job."

It was my goal to be myself in preaching, and more especially, the ministry arena. I was not satisfied to parrot someone else, I wanted to be a female Pastor who challenged the status quo and found my place as one who stood for justice. I was tremendously influenced by the Rev. Dr. Renita Weems, Dr. Katie Cannon, Dr. Delores Williams, all Womanist Theologians, and Elizabeth Schussler Fiorenza, Feminist Theologian whom I met through studies at Perkins. These women challenged my thinking and influenced the way that I understand the word of the Lord, because they often gave voice to women and revealed new thoughts on the Biblical text. Emerging from seminary, I knew that I would not follow a well beaten path, but would journey my own road, trusting our Lord and Savior. Upon returning to Dallas, as a person in Second Chair, I had to carve my way into the fabric of this gigantic community, not by following the beaten path, but strategically striving to move forward, doing things differently.

And yes, I did do them differently. I preached sermons that faced the social ills of the community always using the Revised Common Lectionary, as Dr. Holmes always did. And I attempted to model his style of preaching, that was to tell of a traumatic action that had taken place in the community and bring the text to wrap around the issue. I walked with Sisters who were breast cancer survivors, and spent time in the homes of the community where families had not received communion. It was my responsive way of trying to model discipleship when I preached about issues of Domestic Violence and would be hugged by men and women who whispered "thank you" in my ear. And when the church family knew that I would be taking a much deserved vacation, they would hug me and slip money in my hands to assure that I would have a good time. I was chauffeured to my preaching engagements and always supported by loving sisters. And even on Men's Day, there would be roses hung on my door as a show of support for me as their leader too. And there were meals at Country Clubs and home cooked soul food dinners, and invitation to special events and on birthdays, gifts were slipped under the door of my office. Wow, what a Ride!

My doctoral studies allowed me to move in a different path, at the local church. I would form a committee of persons who would help me to do the work of creating a plan that allowed the church to face the community. And I was told by the Staff Parish Relations Committee that they would pay the tuition for me to attend the Doctor of Ministry Program. Dr. Adams was my Field Advisor for my Project and he was chosen because of his knowledge and commitment to the work of Kingdom Building. My Academic Advisors were, Dr. Joerg Reiger and Dr. Harold J. Recinos. Dr. Reiger was chosen because he was a perfectionist and I knew he would assure that my work was academic. Also, during a time in class, he shared that his mother was a local preacher in Germany. I chose Dr. Recinos because of some of his written works, particularly, *"Jesus Weeps,"* and *"Good News from the Barrio,"* which were foundational to my Project.

This Project work was to be modeled after a community in Boston, Massachusetts as shared through a book, *"Streets of Hope - The Rise and Fall of an Urban Neighborhood"* written by Peter Medoff and Holly Sklar. I traveled to Boston along with Mrs. Gloria Walker to visit the community organization featured in the book, and to learn that a church was the center of the change that had taken place in their community. Likewise, at the center of our work would be some of the indigenous leaders of the Hamilton Park Community Center, a concept that I learned from the Shalom Communities. I would attend the Hamilton Park Community meeting to learn of the issues that were negatively impacting their community and invited their thinking around the Project. A part of my plan was to get all of the churches of the Hamilton Park Community to join together and I had established a Team of Ministers. It was also my goal to have each one share in addressing some of the particular issues. We held a community meeting at the church and invited the Dallas City Council Representative to attend and more than 200 persons were in attendance. I was truly excited. We had meetings and set goals with our Team, however, in the Fall of 2003, I was told that I would take a mid-year appointment to the St. Luke Community UMC.

What would this move mean for my project? I quickly met with the Faculty, Academic Advisors and Field Supervisor and told them of what was happening in my appointment and they assured me that my work was complete. I had met with the Hamilton Park Community Center Leaders, taken a survey of the community, met with the Pastors to form a working team, and was busy drafting my plan for moving forward. They all agreed that the final work to be done was to be the writing. I could complete that in another location. I was not excited about this move, because it was my intent for us to begin to focus on engaging many of the congregational ministries in leadership roles throughout the church.

It was one of the saddest days of my life when I was forced to announce to the congregation that I would be leaving them. And the day of my final sermon, the women got together and decided to wear black. I knew nothing of this plan. When I preached, the Women's Choir, who would follow me to other congregations when I received an invitation, sang on that Sunday. I will never forget that they sang for me, "For Every Mountain," written by Kurt Karr. It was the open door song and when I went down to extend the opportunity for Christian Discipleship, the Senior Pastor anointed me as a sending forth. It was then that all of the women came forth to surround me. Although I was kneeling at the altar and could not see them, I felt the presence of my sisters and saw them when I stood up.

I joined the staff of St. Luke in a mid-year appointment, in October 2003 because the new Senior Pastor of the Hamilton Park Church wanted a change. This midyear move placed me in a precarious position because it was soon time to return to school as I was completing my preparatory for my graduate school project, and the focus was the Hamilton Park community and they had been paying the tuition. This was also a difficult time for me, because I had great love, affinity and connections with the members of the church. The memories of that night before the SPRC are forever burned in my memories. I left the meeting where I had been forced to tell the Committee that I was leaving because the St. Luke church needed me. It was all untrue and when I left the meeting, following the District Superintendent telling them that he had another woman present that he was appointing to my position. That night, I left in tears and spoke with no one. I was humiliated and deeply hurt.

St. Luke Community UMC was pastored at the time by the Rev. Tyrone Gordon. The move had been a lateral one, but because Rev. Gordon was a Pastor who wanted a trained staff, and he had a budget to support it, we traveled. We attended the Schuller Institute, the Proctor Conference, the Black Methodist for Church Renewal Conference in March each year. Our expenses were taken care of an each of us received a stipend. And yes, an appointed Elder of the Church, I received housing. I was appointed to serve along with three other full-time Associate Pastors. And my work area was limited to Congregational Care. I visited the sick and shut-ins and was responsible for assuring that all of the homebound individuals received Holy Communion monthly. However, since I was the only female Clergy, I attached myself to the Women's Ministries of the church, both the United Methodist Women and the Status and Role of Women. I found myself fully engaged with the Prayer Ministry. We met on Saturday mornings and arrived early on Sunday to pray for the early arriving worshippers. We were a faithful ministry group and we believed in the power of prayer. We wrapped our arms around the Pastor and other Clergy each Sunday as we prepared to attend worship. Additionally, I became a member of the Senior Adult Bible Study and organized a Friday Noon Bible Study which we named Power Lunch Bible.

Pastor Gordon had assured me that St. Luke would continue to pay my tuition, however, whenever he turned in the paperwork for approval, the Business Manager rejected it. It was almost time for me to register for the next semester and the previous semester had not been paid. The school informed me that I would not be able to register until the previous semester had been paid. God has always been my place of refuge, and as the old Gospel song would share, "Where could I go, but to the Lord." No money. But God. I turned 55 in March and my City of Dallas Retirement Funds became available. The first check was enough to pay for the past semester, and the next month, the same amount arrived for the next semester. Thank you Jesus. "He's an On-time God, yes He is."

Throughout my life, I found myself making unique connections with the Sisters of Delta Sigma Theta. It had always been my goal to join, however, my life had been too busy. However, in the year 2004, I began my journey to Sisterhood with the North Dallas Suburban Alumnae Chapter. In April of the year I was scheduled to graduate with my Doctorate, my dream became a reality. Along with 25 other dynamic women, we met all requirements. I requested and was pinned by Mrs. Farris Sharp, my mentor and retired Dallas Independent School Principal with whom I had volunteered with as PTA President years earlier. Wow What A Ride!!

It was time to purchase a new cap and gown and stole to be proudly worn as a Doctoral graduate. And a party to be planned because I was never going to graduate again. My family came for my graduation, along with a host from Hamilton Park United Methodist Church and St. Luke Community UMC. They had all been so much a part of my studies. Dr. and Mrs. Adams were there and I must say that without their Advising and support of hiring an editor for my paper I might not have made the December graduation. I was told by my academic advisor that my work was complete, however, I needed an editor to review my written text. That was more money that I did not have. My field advisor, Dr. Jim Adams said, she will hire one. He told me, you will get a check in the mail to cover the cost of the recommended advisor. The next day the check arrived. Wow!

After the completion of the editing, I sat down on my personal computer to make all of the recommended changes and took the finished work to my Advisors, Dr. James Adams, Dr. Harold Recinos and Dr. Joerg Reiger and secured each of their signatures. I was so proud, and the work would not have been complete without the work of my friend, Rev. Terri Phillips who developed the graphs for my manuscript. I am eternally grateful for her work, because I had no idea how to develop graphs, but they were needed to reflect the work that I had done in community.

On the night of my graduation in December 2004, I was seated in one of the rooms with graduate students from all programs at Southern Methodist University. In lieu of a graduation at the Highland Park UMC, it was held "on the hill." There were thousands of us from a variety of programs, but those who had obtained a "Doctorate Degree" were at the head of the line. I was one of three from the theology program. When we were ushered forward, and my name was called, in my highest heels, I marched forward and received my diploma. Wow!! My friend, Mrs. Nellie Thompson, a member of the Staff Parish Relations Team and "famed" Sunday School Teacher of the Hamilton Park Church said, "The moment your name was called, we saw your feet step out like a soldier and you marched across that stage." Wow! What an honor to have my name called by and degree signed by Dr. Gerald Turner, President, Dr. William B.

Lawrence, Dean of Perkins School of Theology, Gerald J. Ford, Board of Trustees, and Ross C. Murfin, Provost.

In the year 2004, on a Sunday morning at St. Luke during the welcoming period, a member of the congregation walked up to me and shared a photo of me. She said, "Look at what I found in the newspaper this morning." It was an 8 X 10 of me. It was the advertisement campaign that I was invited to participate in on behalf of Dallas County Community College. I had been nominated by, Ruby Miller, a member of Hamilton Park, and honored to become the title of Distinguished Alumnus for Cedar Valley College. Dallas County Community College was hosting a campaign entitled, "It all Began Here." I had now earned by Doctorate Degree from SMU Perkins School of Theology and that qualified me to be a recipient. Wow!

The Campaign included Distinguished Alumnus being on radio, television, in movie theaters and billboards. I knew that we had been invited to a studio to do photographs, and to an office to do radio spot interviews, however, I did not know the full extent of the campaign. One day I received a call from Rev. Dr. Sheron Patterson, "Ouida I am going down 35 and I see your picture on a billboard." I could not believe it. The next day one of my daughter, Libbie's friend called to share with her that she had seen me on the screen at the Movie Theater in Cedar Hill. What! I invited my husband to come to the movies with me and I did not tell him about what we were about to see. As the Cinemark Theater was doing its advertisement, up on the big screen was Me. "Can you believe it?" I asked my husband.

Wow! And I will not forget the day that I was shopping at Dillards at Red Bird Mall and I heard my voice sharing what it meant to attend a local Junior College, the low tuition cost and the convenience of classes and the opportunity to live at home. Nobody could imagine the joy that the Campaign gave me as I had been removed from the Pastoral position that I so love. Makes me want to sing with Dottie Peoples, "He's an on time

God, yes He is. He may not come when you want him, but He'll be right there on time. He's an on time God, yes He is."

Immediately following graduation, I received a call from my friend the Reverend Nannette Davis. She shared with me that she was going to Greece to walk the footsteps of Paul and asked if I would accompany her. Her husband had recently died, but had purchased this trip and needed someone to accompany her. Wow, what a great graduation trip. I paid all fees and we were off to Greece.

We flew into Athens and traveled to our hotel where we would join a group from the United States. Our travel was by bus; however, we spent a day on our own seeing the sites around the Athens. Outside of our hotel window we could see the Parthenon, and we could hardly wait to visit. "Mars Hill" is in Athens, the place Paul made his infamous speech, Acts 17:22, where he discussed Jesus with people who believed in Greek gods and goddess'. As other travelers climbed up, I too insisted that I climb up, but coming down was a different story. I was scared, and my feet had become very slippery because of the dirt on top of the hill. We ascended the Acropolis where I noticed that the Greek goddesses were missing. After a full day of sightseeing, we prepared for our trek around the Grecian Countryside by motor coach. We traveled with MTS Travel, one of the leading companies that sponsors Missionary trips.

We toured sites with limited artifacts for our viewing, but still shared the story of our ancient Biblical history. As we arrived near the ancient city of Corinth, we crossed an Isthmus that adjoined the Adriatic and Aegean Seas. The Isthmus is the connector to both seas, and the ships have to be towed through in order to connect with the next sea. It was there that we saw the Church that Paul established in the city of Corinth. And an altar in the city that was dedicated to the Unknown God. High on the hill above the ancient city is the Ancient Temple of Aphrodite (where prostitutes were worshiped)

We traveled to Philippi, the place of Lydia's Baptism. The river is now a small trickling stream, however, there is a modern baptistery located on the site. We arrived there on a very cold morning. The sky was blue and extremely cold. I was asked by our tour leader to do a devotional on site. I was humbled and honored to share a few words of inspiration with our travel companions as I stood near the Baptismal Font located in a building.

I learned that the city of Thessalonica is now the modern city of Thessaloniki. It is a coastal city and as we traveled along we saw a path that the Apostle Paul might have walked as he visited those cities. One of the final places that we visited was a Holy Trinity Monastery of Meteora, where we were told the Apostle Paul spent his last days. It is located on the top of a high hill and in order to get into the Monastery we had to walk 91 steps upward. The curtains in the inner sanctum we were told were so fragile that we could not take pictures.

Rev. Gordon invited the St. Luke Church to take a Mission Trip to Africa. Did someone say travel to Africa? I heard that, our church's Mission this year would be an outreach to Africa University. I began to pack my bags, I could hardly wait. We had more than 75 people sign up for this trip. We departed Dallas and traveled by Delta to Atlanta. From Atlanta we traveled to Heathrow where we spent the night. Our overnight delay was due to a bombing in downtown London. We departed Heathrow at 5:30 p.m. the next day on Zimbabwe Air and arrived the next morning at 5:30 at Harare International airport. The flight from London had African pilots, stewardess, and our 98 percent of the passengers were either African, or African American. When we arrived, the airport served us a full made to order breakfast. We were not allowed to take any photos in the airport. We had to remember the experience in our minds.

Later on the day of our arrival we were picked up by a variety of modes of transportation and taken into the city of Harare, another place that we were not allowed to take pictures. Our leader for this leg of the journey was Mr. James Sally. The next day, we boarded two buses for travel to Africa University. We were stopped every few miles and were inspected, having to reveal our passports. We finally arrived at the campus and had to unload our luggage for the campus. It was the spring of the year for Africa and a bit cool. We thoroughly enjoyed our time there. One experience that I had was to travel into the city to support the Nurses in our midst at an AIDS Clinic. My responsibility was to cheer the persons who were arriving for service. We had very interesting conversations as I sat with the patients and their children as they awaited service.

Oh, I should remind you that one of the hotels that we visited in Africa was the Elephant Hills Hotel. My roommate was Mrs. Carrie Marshall.

She was delightful and we shared many laughs. I was terribly impressed by this hotel, because it was one of the first where I actually found a bath towel that entirely covered my body. We were so excited to be there and though there were shutters on our windows we opened them so that we could see outside. And we actually opened the window. Later, Sister Carrie said, "Pastor Ouida, have you seen this notice?" I drew close and read, "Please do not open the windows, the orangutans and monkeys are playful and will come in." We immediately shut the windows and the shutter and never opened them again.

That evening a trip had been planned for us, we were going to sail down the Zambezi River, I remember hearing about this river on the old Tarzan movies. I was too excited, because until this time we had not seen any animals. We set sail later in the evening as the sun was setting, and I had my camera ready to take pictures. There was an elephant on the side of the river that was not in full view, and I can't begin to tell you all of the pictures that I took in order to get a picture of the elephant. When we arrived back to shore, I was walking the gang plank when two orangutans crossed my path fighting. I was scared, but could not run back because someone was behind me. And when we got off the vessel, there were monkeys everywhere, looking at us. They were uncaged and roaming free. Wow!!

The next stop was Victoria Falls, which is located within the Victoria Falls National Park. When we toured the Park and anyone who got close enough to the edge of the Falls, a rainbow would appear behind them. I have now learned that the Falls protects the mouth and east bank of the Zambezi River. And I stood there, overlooking the massive Falls, too afraid to get too close because the edge was slippery. Wow!!

This was the beginning of our Africa experience. We were off to a safari to Chobe National Park and on our way we saw giraffes grazing in the distance. A family of elephants were crossing the road and we had to stop and await their passage. What a difference a day makes. When we got to the border of the Chobe National Park we had to again show our passports and go through the process of cleaning our shoes so that we would not bring any germs into the Park. We then go into open air jeeps and rode through the park. We saw more giraffes, impalas, monkeys, African birds, and at the waters' edge, we saw hippopotamus and other unnamed strange creatures. Then there was a tour where we saw the most beautiful crocodile and I was happy to be on the top deck of the boat. And more elephants than one can imagine. And yes, there was a visit to Soweto. Though we were not permitted to take pictures, the visit is forever embedded in my mind. We visited the home of some of the citizens, they were tiny which I have now learned were homes built near the Gold mines to accommodate the Africans.

This was the time of great loss of lives for African people due to the AIDS Pandemic. The United Methodist Church had established houses for the children of those lost to AIDS and it was in a located in the Old Mutare Mission. We visited the Mission and some of the homes along with the house parents and the children. St. Luke had actually purchased a grinder for the meal that was grown on the campus of the University and we were privileged to see where it was established. Another mission opportunity that I shared was to help organize the many book donations that were made to the University. The early evenings were filled with worship and the opportunity to hear the famed Africa University Choir singing. Later we would gather in the dormitories and share board games. Our meals were served in the University Cafeteria, along with the students. We learned to adjust our eating habits as we sat with and shared the food that was served to the students on campus.

The students were very committed to the learning process and they had very committed faculty and staff. On the campus there is represented all of the various tribes of Africa, and we were told that if there was ever to be a total unification of Africa, the University would be the center of it. That is because when the students arrive at the University, the have to learn to speak English so that everyone can communicate. There are many languages spoken in Africa, French, Portuguese, and Swahili to name a few. And they have the largest constituency of church in the whole of the United Methodist Church.

While we were there another part of the Mission was to visit churches on a Sunday morning. The Pastor of the church where I attended was pastored by Rev. Faith. There were more than 500 people in the church. As we were driving up, people were coming from every direction walking to the church. She shared with us that she had established a mission to make the men of the Church Evangelist. And on the Sunday that we were there, she Commissioned several men for the work of Ministry. I also had the opportunity to share in the Baptismal Service in which several families were baptized. She used the method of pouring, as I lay hands on the heads of each person. She had a new church building, because she shared with us that since her name was "Faith" she had asked God in faith for a new building and God had provided. The old shack of the old church stood outside as a memento of what God had done. There were hundreds of children and the Women's Mission were dressed in uniforms and all of the children participated in the service by beating drums and other musical beats during worship. I reminded of Psalm 150 – Praise god in his sanctuary; praise him in his mighty heavens. Praise him for his acts of power; praise him for his surpassing greatness....praise him with timbrel and dancing, praise him with strings and pipe, praise him with clash of cymbals, praise him with resounding cymbals. Let everything that has breath, praise the Lord."

Back on the campus of the University, every evening the students sang and we listened. We did not understand the language, but they were giving praise to our God and we enjoyed it. And it was great getting to know the students on the campus. One shared with us that her parents had sent her to the University because she was crippled and they knew that she would not likely get married. She said her family used all of their resources to send her to school and she was unable to go home. She said that she had to stay there year round for four years. She said when her mother arrived for her graduation, she could not contain herself. Her words were, "I tried not to think about my parents so that I could do my studying, but when I saw my mother, I could not contain myself. I cried and I hugged my mother." I could only imagine the reunion with her mother, but even more the pride in her success.

During my final year at St. Luke, we were invited to take a ministry trip to Brazil with another Rev. Carlos. Of course I was interested, I had always loved to travel and wanted to see the world. I had no idea that the Church would be the center of my travels. When we arrived in Foz de Iguazu, we were meet by some of the citizens and welcomed to their country. We were not fully aware of all that would be expected of us. However, Pastor Gordon was going to be the Preacher for a Revival in the country. He would be interpreted by Rev. Carlos … On a bus tour through the city, we began to sing songs, and someone suggested that we sing Oh Happy Day. When it came time for the verse, I started to sing, I thought it was all for fun. However, on the first night of the Revival, Minister of Music Monya Logan and the choir began to sing the chorus to Oh Happy Day and she nodded for me to do the verse. I sang it, and then, Pastor Gordon kicked in on the refrain. Without our knowledge, we were recorded and Oh Happy Day became our song for the season. Everywhere we went, we were requested to sing it. It was a joyful song and though we enjoyed it, we vowed never to sing it again upon our return home.

One of the ministries that we were very engaged with on this trip were the Orphanages. One night we went to an Orphanage with more than 100 children inside. The children were very thin. It was a rainy night, and as we were shown around the Orphanage, we saw wet clothes hanging around the building. We learned from the Priest that they did not have a working dryer. When I got back to the bus, I shared with Pastor Gordon and our members that my heart had been so touched and I thought that we needed to take a collection to be shared with them. Everyone chipped in and we called the Priest aboard our bus and shared with him the offering. His words to us were, "Thank you, we would not have food tonight, except for the donation from you all." We pledged then that our Easter Offering would be shared with them to purchase a dryer for the Orphanage.

Standing at the feet of
Jesus - Rio

The hotel that we lived in was in Rio de Janerio, right on the ocean. I would exercise and look out the window to the beautiful site. Wow, our God is awesome. However, it is important that I mention that whenever we traveled, we had security with us. Although we never experienced any problems, it was easy to see that we were in a country with its' own set of problems. We would come down from our rooms in the morning and find little girls sleeping on towels on the streets. And we were warned not to get too close to people or we could become victims of crime. During the day we would travel to see many sites in the city, the Jesus on the cross and a breathtaking sight on our way up of the entire area of Rio, while on the train trip up. I never made it to Sugar Loaf, I have my limitations, but I stood at the feet of Jesus. And as one traveled through the cities, it was easy to see the differences in how people lived. On one side of the freeway, plush apartments and condominiums. On the other side, the squalors. People were literally stacked on top of each other in rooms without walls.

The Orphanages were not very different. Children were being kept off the streets, but the means of support was quite limited. My heart was so deeply touched when I was told about a set of twins who had been born with AIDS and when the parents learned of their condition took them to an Orphanage. Those were saddest babies that I saw, never a smile on their faces, only sadness. Can you imagine being abandoned by your parents? Helpless! Alone! What could St. Luke do?

We pledged to make a difference. And when we returned home, we raised the money to purchase a dryer for the Orphanage and I was sent  along with Ed Patterson, Lay Leader to deliver the gifts to Rio. When we arrived I was invited to share on a local television station why we had come to their country. However, when we went to see where the dryers had been placed, it was a different location. Our Lay Person became indignant and we both insisted that the dryers be delivered to the place where we designated them. Reluctantly they were delivered to the right place. The rationale for the different placement was, the other Orphanage had received a dryer.

Whenever we traveled, we always found a time for some fun. The first visit, we went to the Iguazu Falls and observed them from the top. We watched as some adventurous persons rode the falls beneath. I said to myself, those people are crazy, I would never find myself riding the Falls. The second trip, we were taken to the bottom of the Falls, and guess who rode the Falls? Yes, it was the most adventurous thing that I have ever done. The driver of the boat drove us right into the falls at a high rate of speed, but backed us out very slowly. Wow! This was another parts of God's magnificent creation.

During my second year under appointment, I became appointed as the Senior Associate Minister on the Team and was assigned to work with the Administrative Ministries of the Church. Since St. Luke had a Business Manager, my work in this area was limited. I loved the music of the St. Luke Church, they had dynamic choirs and a diversity of music. I love to sing and though I never attended choir rehearsal, I tried to sing every song along with the choir. But even more than singing, the Music Ministry included the Liturgical Dancers of every age, including the Senior Citizens. There were dynamic music programs with guest on special occasions, i.e. Christmas, Easter and African American History Month always provided opportunities for the different genre musical ministries to share in the worship.

My preaching time was limited at the St. Luke Church and as one who loved to preach, after three years, I asked the Bishop Rhymes Moncure to please find a church to send me to. His response to me was, "Ouida, I am looking for you a place." I learned that asking for a move, one never knows what on will receive. One day as I sat in my office, a Clergy sister walked in and told me that she was taking my place. I responded, "Oh, I didn't know that I was leaving." She had already been told that she would be taking my place and I had not been told that I was leaving. Wow.

Appointment to United Methodist Church of the Disciple

I was told by the District Superintendent that I would have a seating at the United Methodist Church of the Disciple. The Superintendent asked me to arrive about 6 p.m. and remain in my car. I almost left, because it was 9:30 before I was invited in. This was going to be a Cross-Racial appointment and it appeared that the Superintendent had to convince the church that I was being seated there. When I was introduced, I noticed the faces around the table. There was one African Male and one African American Female, and 5 or 6 Caucasians and the chair was Native American, some that I never saw again after the introduction.

The next week, I was invited to lunch by an Anglo member of the congregation and the Local Pastor (African American) who was appointed there. The Caucasian wanted to share with me that they were thinking about selling the Parsonage. She was not a member of SPRC and had appointed herself to advise me that I might not want to move into the house. I shared with her that I would be moving into the house, if I only stayed one night.

The Church of the Disciple had been established by the Reverends Matt and Camille Gaston in 1993, as a Multi-Cultural Congregation. They built a new establishment and moved in around 1999. Upon my arrival, the 250 member congregation was 97 percent Anglo with a sprinkling of African Americans and Hispanics, along with one Native American, and the community was going through a tremendous demographic change. The building was a $1.5 million plant and the note for the building and the Parsonage was $7,000 per month. My daughter had been hired as musician for the congregation years earlier and was still playing for the church when I arrived in 2006. As the people walked away, I spent my days walking the neighborhoods passing out invitations to others to come and worship with us.

When I prepared to leave the St. Luke Church, the District advised me that I would not receive funding for moving, so I called the Church of the Disciple to see if they would help me my materials moved to the new location. Spencer Smith was a young Anglo Student Minister appointed to the church and he agreed to take the van and move my things to COD. Upon my arrival, when I opened the door to the office, and we saw the book shelf, he said, "Where did that old thing come from?" It was rustic and quite dirty. I shared with the Lay Leader, I cannot put my books on that shelf and requested that we purchase some. I was told by the Office Volunteer, "We don't have any money." I asked the Lay leader if I purchase book shelves would he pick them up. His prompt response was. "Yes." The computer was a "dumb terminal" attached to a keyboard. I was shocked.

I went to the local Office Supply and all of the shelves had to be assembled. When I called to have them picked up, there was agreement that they would get someone to put them together. As we prepared for Sunday morning, I asked if we could write a "welcome song" for the worship celebration. The song was written by one of the choir members and was inserted into the worship experience.

It was my first Sunday and many of the members of the St. Luke Church came to worship with me on the first Sunday, the house was filled and the only significant change and maybe a bit of the order, that was made in the worship was the song, but it set off complaints, none of which came to my ears. In staff meeting the following week, I asked if anyone had heard any complaints and Spencer, the Youth Minister said, "Ouida they are ready to kill you." When I heard that they were upset, I apologized to the congregation in worship and changed everything back as it had been. They had already called the Superintendent who showed up in worship the next Sunday. I explained what had happened and it help to calm him down temporarily.....

I did not have time to time to think about those trivial things, I had work to do. When fear rises in one's heart, we had to keep doing what we were doing. I had learned that faith is not the absence of fear, but it is to fear, but do it anyway. Our church was falling apart faster than we could build it up. Therefore, with all of the tools in hand, demographic information, statistics, we had to research the numbers and attempt to minister in this field. The challenge was, there is need for money in order to do effective ministry and every dollar that we brought in had to be paid out – salaries, pension, insurance, housing, Church Note and Parsonage.

I was finally a Senior Pastor again. I was ready to present my vision for us moving forward. I have learned a few things since that time. First of all, the congregation did not see me as their Pastor and I was attempting to move them forward too quickly. And I was an African American woman, many did not want a woman for a Pastor, nor an African American. And this was a very religiously conservative community. The only two other women Pastors in the City, both were white one at FUMC DeSoto and the other had about 20 members. Though the NTC was attempting to make some strides in Cross-racial appointments, only one had been successful at this time and it was in a more progressive community on the north side of Dallas. Congregations had not been trained how to support people of color, both male and female and most of those appointments did not last a year. I was appointed and forgotten, but I never asked to be moved. I knew that if we were to make changes in the way things were being done, someone had to stand. I was not a part of the Civil Rights movement of the 1960's because I lived in the country and my small town was not engaged. But if I had to make comparison with the way that I was treated, it was quite similar.

There were those who simply dismissed me and everything that I preached. My sermons became the subject of blogs and discussions to which I was not privy. When I attempted to change my preaching style to more lecture, I was told by one parishioner, "It does not matter to me what you say, you can't tell me anything." I questioned, where is the Christianity in that? I made myself content with preaching the lectionary and about the love of Jesus and all I got were cold stares.

On the third Sunday of June, I preached my first sermon to the congregation. As tradition, the members of St. Luke came to support me. We made a slight change in the order of the service and I asked them to add a welcome song. I was almost thrown out of the church. The new Superintendent came to worship and told me that I was destroying the church. I told him that when I learned that the change disturbed the people, I had already changed it back. It was easy to see that I did not have any support from the Conference. Within two weeks of my arrival, I met with the Finance Committee and they told me that the church had no money. This was not a poor church. There were two physicians, nurse practioner and two other RN's, three lawyers, Federal Government employees, a Print company owner, Police Officer, Service Advisor, Teachers, Bankers, College Administrator, Business Administrators, and other small business owners and managers. They were not poor, but this was a tactic to get the Bishop to move me. Therefore, I told them to ask each Family to give $1000 to rebuild the budget. Their response to me was, "You have not been here long enough to ask the member to do anything like that." I said, "Okay, what is your suggestion?" They had no answers.

We met the following Sunday after worship for the meeting of the Administrative Council. Each Team member shared their report and when it came to the Finance, they shared that the church has no money. I spoke and shared my suggestion with them. And I shared with the Council, "You all are aware that you have not paid me my first paycheck. However, I would never ask you to do anything that I am not willing to do first." I wrote a check for $1000 and laid it on the table and sat and looked at each of them. The room was completely silent, except for the tearing of the checks. At the end the Finance Team counted the money and we received $17,000 from that offering.

This was a time of antitheses, it was the best of times and the worst of times. Immediately upon my arrival African American Families began to join the church. Within four months of my arrival, we had added 40 new members to the congregation. Simultaneously, I was told that I was to host a 6:30 a.m. Bible Study for a group and when I arrived and asked what they were studying, they looked and me and said "That's up to you." I shared what I was preparing for my sermon on Sunday and no one shared a word. And after two months, everyone got to busy to attend early morning study. My beginning at the Church was to be a constant challenge. There was no cultural sensitivity. I invited the congregational leaders to the Parsonage for a visit and they shared, we want to grow, but not so fast. In actuality, when the African American people started coming, the Anglos dropped out. Many of them joined the Methodist Church of Ovilla. And each week, I would receive a really sarcastic letter from the Pastor as he made us aware that a few more of our congregation that had joined his.

The former Pastor's wife would come over each week and conduct a class for a group of young Anglo women who no longer attended worship. Our church paid a babysitter to keep her kids while she did so. I informed the Superintendent about this action and he said, she was only trying to help. Her new congregation was more than 50 miles away and she was driving it each week to meet with her friends. It was only when I shared with one of her friends who was the leader of the group that I thought that she should stay and help her husband and his new congregation. It was apparent that she had shared my words, because she wrote a letter to me, with copies to be sent to the Bishop, District Superintendent and my SPRC. Only then did he take action and told the former Pastor that his wife should not come back to the church. And neither did the little group. These were very stressful times and I seemed to have no one to lean on, except Jesus. "Where Could I Go But to the Lord?"

It was during this time that our Bishop Moncure died. Since he left an unfulfilled term, Bishop Alfred Norris was appointed to fill in. I visited him and he shared with me, "Ouida, I knew that some of the people would leave, but not so fast." I kept preaching the Lectionary text and using the words of Theologian Karl Barth, "the Bible must be read in one hand and the newspaper in the other," but many see that as social action. However, when I read the Bible that is exactly what I see that Jesus did, confront, intervene and teach through faithful acts for the betterment of society.

We organized an Evangelism Team, led by Deborah Sharp and together with her husband Keith, and a few others we spent our Saturdays

interfacing with others in the community. It was my intent to make use of my doctoral work for establishing ministries within the church. We were outwardly focused, offering programs that we believed and according to the demographics of the community would meet the needs of our community. When we learned that there were a considerable number of single female households, we attempted to offer programs that address issues that had been raised in the survey. One major drawback was that according to the demographics, this was a religiously conservative community. And there were times that we would have visitors ask, "Where is the Pastor's husband?" And when they were told he does not attend church here, they never returned.

Deborah Sharp
& Terria Jones

When we learned of the number of teen pregnancies within the schools, we offered a "Purity Course" led by Daphne Lusk and a Team of parents. The course was 8 weeks long and included health information, as well as spiritual grounding. When we learned that some of the children were coming to school without school supplies, we hosted a "Back to School Festival" giving away school supplies, demonstrating how the children were to dress, as well as having Administrators from the District explain some of the expectations for the school year. In addition to opening our doors for flu shots in the fall season, we hosted an Annual Health Fair that was ultimately combined with the Back to School Festival. Deborah Sharp, our Community Nurse, led this annual event that included bringing on site the Fire Truck for the children, mammograms and prostrate screening for the parents, and local vendors to showcase their businesses. Bible Study was held on Wednesdays with the summers being the most popular times because the entire family could study together.

The Easter Season was very special for our church. For several years we held an Easter Extravaganza on the parking lot of our church, complete with an Easter bunny for a photo opportunity. The children and youth loved this time because in lieu of real eggs, we stuffed our eggs with candy. We would gather on the Wednesday prior to the event and stuff the eggs, some with money and according to age groups, we would allow the children to hunt for the eggs. This was another season for the church to be decorated with Easter Lilies that were provided by the members of the congregation.

We loved the season of Fasting. Solemn programs were held as we prepared for the celebration. We observed the penitential season with Fasting from –Ash Wednesday through Easter Sunrise, exclusive of the Sundays. We would worship on Ash Wednesday and everyone would make a commitment of what they were giving up for the season. One of our members would suggest that in lieu of giving up something, we could take up something, i.e. journaling, meditating, reading the Bible daily. Easter Week was filled with activity, Maundy Thursday with the seder meal. On Good Friday the congregation shared the seven Last Words of Jesus from the cross, sometime with guest preachers and at other times with the Lay Members of the congregation. Easter Sunday, was always a very special time with the congregants. We would arrive for Sunrise Service at 5:30 and then Break the Fast with a meal together. The Liturgical Dancers would always usher us into the Praise Celebration at 8 and 10 a.m. Wow! "Oh how good and pleasant it is when God's people live together in unity!" Psalm 133:1 (NIV).

When congregations are small and funds are limited there has to be vision and motivation to keep the people moving ahead. The congregation was always surrounded by prayer and we always express faith as the core of our sustenance and existence. And the Bible teaches, "Faith without works is dead," James 2:17. These are not merely words that are found in Scripture; they are words that should become application for our lives. Life is not filled with easy answers, but often is complicated by the things that we face, real and relational. We cannot afford to give up when difficulties come in our lives, but we have to lean on the teachings of Scripture. Sometimes it requires that we look back to see how far our God has bought us. Life is not without its struggles, but when we have God as the anchor for our souls, we don't stand still and look for handouts. We press forward with belief in the God we have been taught about, believing that with God all things are possible. These are not words that we employ if we have simply heard about God. These are the words of those who have encountered difficulties in life and did not give up.

For our church, faith was more than an expression because we also realized that, "Faith is the substance of things hoped for and the evidence of things not seen," Hebrews 11:1. And there were quotes that I lived by and encouraged the congregation to make their own. One of my favorites is in the words of the poem "Don't Quit," written by John Greenleaf Whittier, "Success is failure turned inside out– The silver tint of the clouds of doubt, And **you** never can tell how **close you** are, It **may** be near when it seems so far, So stick to the fight **when you**'re **hardest hit**– It's when things seem worst that **you must not quit**." Trudging through life's hardships is difficult, but there has to be a soft core at your center, a place of implicit trust in God. God promises, "I will never leave you, nor forsake you," Deuteronomy 31:6. Those are the words of Moses spoke to Joshua when he was 120 years of age and turned leadership of the Israelites over to him. The truths of the bible come to encourage us and are not limited generationally. I learned this truth from the Prayer Ministry of the Hamilton Park UMC, "God is not a man, that he should lie; neither the son of a man, that he should repent, hath he said, and shall he not do it? Or hath he spoken, and shall he not make it good?" Wow! A call to a walk of faith.

We only had faith, not enough money. Not enough help. Not enough believers. Faith as we sat around the Administrative Council table and listened to our financial report. If only, I could get the entire congregation to believe in this faith. I am a tither, and I encouraged tithing. However, if you do not have the faith to believe what God can and will do for those who trust in God, you may never know the blessings of the promise, "**Bring ye all the tithes into the storehouse**, that there may be meat in mine house, and prove me now herewith, saith the LORD of hosts, if I will not open you the windows of heaven, and pour you out a blessing, that there shall not be room enough to receive it," Malachi 3:10. This is not an instantaneous return on investment that you will receive the next week, or month. Neither is it playing the stock market, It is again, trusting God and taking God at God's word. It is being faithful through difficult times and trusting that God will see us through. The congregation tried tithing, but when they did not see instant returns, they waivered in their commitment. But those of us who had survived many storms, understood and remained steadfast. We had to do additional fundraisers in order to secure that all financial obligations were met. And I believe that we really came to understand what it means, "we then that are strong ought to bear the infirmities of the weak," Romans 15:1."

I must share that I believe these words. Based upon the challenges that I have faced in life, unwavering faith is a mandate for those of us on this journey of life. For me these words are not spoken from a place of ease. Although I had spoken words of comfort so many times before for persons who had lost loved ones, it was now my time. It was during the second year of my appointment, on Thanksgiving weekend. My only, John C. Lee, III, the gregarious young man who spent far too many years at Grambling State University, but graduated. My baby who had been diagnosed in 2000 with bipolar disorder. The son whose desire it was to go to New Orleans for the Bayou Classic, met his destiny on Lancaster Road, not more than a mile from home.

The week had been tumultuous, we knew that he was in a manic phase and did not want him to drive his car for fear of what would happen on the roadway. The dealership where he had purchased the car had it remotely locked, however, on the Friday following Thanksgiving, he called and told them that he was coming to pay his past due note. They unlocked the car and he packed his clothes for the journey. I had spoken to him not more than 30 minutes before and wanted to get him help. And on my way to the Parsonage that day, I almost exited. I believe that it was the Holy Spirit that directed me to keep driving. As soon as I walked in the door, my

husband called and said, "Brace yourself, John has been involved in an accident." I got in the car and drove as fast as I could to Charlton Methodist Hospital, crying all the way and calling family.

When I arrived at the hospital and told them that I was looking for my son, John Lee III, they told me to take a seat. I shared "I am a Pastor, they always let me in to see the patients." I knew things were serious, I had heard those words before. The receptionist said "Take a seat, I am going to get someone to speak with you." I started to cry loudly, disturbing everyone else in the lobby that they took to the triage area. And when the Chaplain showed up, I screamed. She told me that they were taking me to the Family Room. I knew then that my son was dead. There were no words that would console me. Shortly afterward, Deborah showed up. The doctors then came in and the words that I knew were probably inevitable, and I did not want to hear, they spoke. "We did everything that we could to save your son." I cried out loudly and my friend attempted to comfort me, but there was no comforting me. "Leave me alone! Don't touch me!" My son, my baby was gone. They shared that they would allow me to see him shortly. One of the physicians asked, "Did he play a tuba?" "Yes, why do you ask?" He replied, "He was holding the mouthpiece in his hand." When I saw his lifeless body, I understood the question. There on his forehead was the blemish that revealed that his head had collided with his mouthpiece. He was gone. I remembered the words from earlier quoted by Sister Mary Paul when I lost my daddy, "the Lord giveth and the Lord taketh away, blessed be the name of the Lord."

When my husband arrived some minutes later, I said to him as he entered the room and sat down. "He is gone." He shouted, "What?" Our beloved son's body lay lifeless in the room next door. My husband's Pastor, the Rev. Dr. A. E. Campbell, came through the door, along with the Rev. Tyrone Gordon, my former Senior Pastor, along with a host of Family and friends. Even as I pen these words, tears are falling from my eyes. It's so hard to say good-bye.

Never had I experienced such pain as a mother. My Pastoral role had to take a back seat. I was the mother of John C. Lee, III and loved him with an undying love. And I cried. I cried because he was dead. I cried because he had developed bipolar disorder. I cried because he so desperately wanted to be a band teacher, but was unable to handle the pressure. I cried for all of the things he tried to do, and was not given the opportunity. But most of all I cried because I loved him. He was my joy. He was my baby, bone of my bone and flesh of my flesh. And I could do nothing, but come to grip with it.

I knew my son was sick and that he refused to take the medicine that would normalize his actions. I remembered the words of comfort that I had spoken to so many. Death does not have the final word. We are people of the Resurrection. I also remembered that our God is the one who heals. And that healing does not always come in life, oftentimes only in death. I recalled that a few weeks prior to his death, our son had been arrested for fighting a teacher at Lancaster Middle School. John was very non-violent, therefore, I concluded that the teacher must have called him crazy. Whatever he said pushed John to the point of reaction. He was never a fighter. Never caused his family any problems. He was loving and kind and would attempt to stop people from fighting. I knew that he was out of control. This may be hard for some to understand, but these are my thoughts. I believe that God did not want our son to ruin his good reputation with abrasive actions. He had been Ordained as a Baptist Minister, almost a year prior to the date of his death. He loved the Lord, singing, preaching and playing his beloved bass guitar. Our God moves in mysterious ways, and I believe that when he died in that horrific crash on Lancaster Road, the Lord said, I will take him home to be with me so that he can be healed.

My faith seems to be simplistic on the surface, but it is imbedded deep within my heart. It did not prohibit the pain of the loss, nor did it dry my tears. However, I managed to get through that time by taking a walk of faith. Every time I cried, I would say to God, "God I love you with all of my heart, and know that I trust you with my son." I would then speak to my son, "John, baby, you know that your mother loves you with all of her heart and I know that I can release you to God." I did not say those words one time, but more times each day than I can count. I was living in the parsonage and my bedroom was upstairs. Every morning I would wake up and hear the birds singing outside in the tree near the window. But now I only heard silence. And one day, I woke up and again I heard the birds singing. I had truly released my son to God. Wow! I am reminded, "Trust in the Lord with all of your heart and lean not to your own understanding. In all of your ways acknowledge God and He will direct your path," Proverbs 3:5-6, and this was one of John's favorite verses. Along with walk by faith and not by sight. He would say to me numerous times, "Mama, don't worry about me, release me to God." I finally did.

The Church family told me to stay home, they would take care of everything. I did for about two months, but the house was beginning to close in on me. And the church was still going through its financial struggles. By now I was assisted by Carolyn Albritton, as Youth Pastor at the church. The Laity did its very best and kept things moving ahead, but I wanted to get back to work. At this time we still had a few of the most faithful Anglos still hanging in there with us. I will never forget, Monica and Steve, who were both so helpful to our church. Monica managed the finances, while Steve was chair of Trustees. Jeff Atwell was one of the faithful and supportive members of SPRC. Scott Perkins who sang with the Male Chorus and his wife Lisa who faithfully decorated our Altar. Lou Ann Richardson and Shirley, were a supportive couple who offered their leadership and financial support to the congregation. And faithful Michael Matthews who served as Usher and Trustee Chair, he never left us, he was a committed Christian who loved his Pastor. Lon and Gloria Cardwell who would share with me that she did not understand the congregation that said it wanted to be Multi-cultural, but could so easily walk away. Mike Pridemore who sang in the Choir and Linda who faithfully Ushered at the door. I am most thankful for them and all the ways that they supported their church through the years. I remember with fondness when we were going through a particularly financially challenging time that Lou Ann Richardson shared with me that she had just received a bonus. She came by my office and handed me a $5000 check to be used however I wanted to use it. The check was immediately turned over to the Finance Committee so that it could be used in support of the Church.

Each year as persons resigned from their positions, it was necessary to replace them with willing servants, many of whom had to be trained. While Steve was serving as chair of Trustee, we learned that the church had a few roof leaks. Steve requested bids for the repairs. The bid that was selected was for $30,000. I questioned how we would be able to afford the repairs. The next week after we received the bid, the City of DeSoto experienced a storm. When the storm hit, I am told by the passersby, the winds lifted the tile and it blew over against the fence. We then called the insurance company and their Claims Adjuster estimated the replacement cost at $72,000. Our deductible was $1000. Needless to say, we got a brand new roof. Wow! I

Women's Day celebrated in May

learned that it pays to be faithful to God and God will take care of you. I am singing, "Be not dismayed, whatever betide, God will take care of you."

It did not take me long to learn that the members who lived in this community took the summers off...and their money along with them. I suggested that since the United Methodist Women's month was celebrated in May, we should celebrate Women's Day. We would ask each woman to donate $100 each in support of our local church budget. The UMW agreed and we raised more than $3500, to be put in the Savings Account in order to bridge us through the summer. Likewise, the United Methodist Men would celebrate Men's Day in June around Father's Day. They too would be solicited for a $100 contribution in support of the summer shortfall. From the men we would usually gather about $1500 making a total of $5,000 to support our summer income.

Men's Day Celebrated in June

Summers were filled with activities for the Family gathering on Wednesday nights for a time of study and reflection on the Word of the Lord. Our Youth Minister, Rev. Carolyn Albritton, who came to us as an Intern from Perkins School of Theology from Southern Methodist University. Later, Rev. Patricia Chapman, and Rev. Carissa Rodgers would work with the Youth. Rev. Cheryl Jones and later Rev. Cori Bell, served as Children Ministers at Church of the Disciple. Each of these women committed to the work of Ministry and made our work a tremendous success. Although we had no money to pay staff, it was such a blessing to be supported by the Internship Program, who paid salary support to each of the students. I served as Mentor to each of the Ministers and we organized a group to support the students as they matriculated their way through seminary. Proverbs 18:24 records, "A man that hath friends must shew himself friendly: Wow!

Pastoring is more than just preaching; it is making connections with the community in which you are appointed to serve. As Senior Pastor in the City of DeSoto, I became a partner to the school district and participated on the Superintendent's Advisory Commission. Church of the Disciple became the Adopter of the Cockrell Hill Elementary School. I served on the campus Advisory Board and was an annual speaker for

Career Days. I even had the privilege of serving as Principal for the Day at another Elementary School. We opened and closed the school year annually with Prayer at the Pole, in which we prayed for the Officials, Board Members, the Student Body and Parents of the community. Through engagement with the DeSoto Police and Clergy, I came to know the Pastors and Community leaders of the community. We partnered with the School District in their annual Back to School Festival at the High School and prayed for the success of the Athletic Department. Association with the Rotary Club further engaged me in the leadership of our community. It was impossible not to get caught up in the politics of the City, especially when the elected officials were your friends. And I deem it very important to become collegial with the Clergy who are in the places of our appointments. We are not to be lone rangers, because we are representative of the Christian Community and we are striving to engage more people in ministry as we strive to build the beloved community. My association with the Pastors of DeSoto and the African American Pastor's Coalition have proven to be a place of strength.

Pastoring is a lonely road, and we should not have to walk it alone. And though the United Methodist Church is world-wide, a small town or a rural community without the collegiality can be a very lonely place. I am reminded of the Scripture found in Psalm 133, "How good and pleasant it is when God's people live together in unity!" It is good to know that we are not, or should not be separated by gender, socio-economic, nor ethnic class. Our God is calling us to unity. We are losing generations of people while we assert ourselves as alt right, supreme or privileged as the people of faith. Those of us who are leaders should not merely talk the talk, but walk the walk. And that is what disturbed me about my final appointment in the United Methodist Church. It did not matter how much I was willing to bend toward the people, they took opposition to me and I believe it was about the fact that I was African American. It appears to me that we have no problem with appointments when the African American woman is subservient, or in a staff position. It is when we are the Senior Pastor, or leader of the congregation that the real problems arise.

Throughout all that I faced as an African American Clergy Woman, I never asked to be moved from this congregation. I thought that we were all Christians, and Christians can work together, respect one another and even when there are differences, we could get past them. It appears that I read that in Scripture, Galatians 3:28, "There is neither Jew nor Greek, there is neither bond nor free, there is neither male or female; for we are all one in Christ Jesus." I shared my struggles with an Anglo female Clergy and she shared that there was a man in her congregation who had led the church through a difficult time of change. She introduced me to him and made plans for him to come to our church and speak with our SPRC. He had developed a real process that had worked well in their church. The Superintendent was invited to participate in the conversation. After listening, he said, "that sounds like a good plan, I'll keep that in mind for some other time." His mind was made up, I was not the proper fit for the congregation.

On the other hand, during the course of my most disappointing moments, I traveled to Philadelphia to attend the Black Methodist for Church Renewal Conference. Those who know me personally are aware of my jovial spirit, but not this time. I was heartbroken and attempting to determine how I was going to make it. We were in the city for five days and every day Bishop Norris would ask, "Ouida, how are you doing?" Each time my response was, "Bishop, I am doing fine." I knew that my face did not show it. I was in pain, disappointed, and hurt, but I have never been one to give up. On the last night of the Conference, I saw down and wrote a letter to the Bishop. My words were, "since I was appointed as Senior Pastor we have added 40 new members to the congregation, our bills are current and so is our apportionment. I am so fully aware that I am an Itinerant Elder of the Church, I do not have appointing authority. I serve at the will of the Bishop and the Cabinet and am willing to go wherever I am sent. My appointment is in your hands."

When I returned home from Philly, I was sitting in my office and noticed a group of cars had gathered on the parking lot. Unofficial leader has appointed themselves to go to see the Superintendent to discuss moving me. On the evening of my birthday, the Superintendent came down to hold a meeting with the disgruntled members. They had all written letter sharing why I should be removed as their Pastor. The Lay Leader said to me, "You need to get the Black people to write letters for you; all the white people are writing letters to get you removed." I talked with a few people, but I will always remember the words of one African American, "I am not writing a letter on your behalf, God has you and you are not going to be moved." Although this was an SPRC meeting, I was told that I could not attend. I sat in my office and awaited the response. He emerged from the meeting and to me that the church was divided and he did not know why I would not just leave. I recall that I had a picture of my granddaughter on a shelf in the room, I pointed to it and said, "My granddaughter has never mentioned that she was called to ministry and may never receive a call, but I am staying for her. Should she ever receive a call to a cross-racial appointment, I want her to know that her grandmother stayed so that she could have an opportunity." He left angrily and I remained in the community for 13 years. There are times that you have to be the change that you want to see. Wow! Was I punished for my willingness to stay? I was never offered another appointment. I believe that "God knows the plans that God has for you, plans to prosper you and to give you a future with hope and not to harm you," Jeremiah 29:11.

Who knew what God had in mind for me, one thing that I do know is that sometimes our lessons and assignments are difficult, but God. As the people walked away, the financial crisis of 2008 hit the DeSoto Community hard for those who had purchased new homes. So many of the citizens lost their jobs, and their homes, but the Preacher/Prophet has to know the difficulties and keep sharing the word as described by Karl Barth, with the newspaper in one hand and the Gospel message in the other. There has to be an intersection of the word and the world in order to share hope and encourage the people to hold onto their faith.

The other challenge that our church faced was there were not enough hands on deck to carry out some of the programs that we proposed. And the finances continued to wane. The Prayer Ministry decided to do an Annual Prayer Breakfast. One of the members, Jannette Gosha made the tickets and we planned the program together. Every member of the Prayer Team sold tickets and on the day of the event, Dr. Thelma Wells was invited to be the speaker. The house was packed and the food was adequately prepared, the Youth served as hostesses. Although it was a fundraiser, it did not have the feel of raising money, it was a very spiritual event. We raised more than $1500 for the church budget. Each of the ministries were aware that the funds that were raised were to be given to the church in support of our shortfall.

The budget was planned by the Finance Team each year; however, based on our experience, we were aware that the budget would not be fulfilled without additional funds. The shortfall was not because the people were not making the money, it was because of a lack of faith to pay their tithes and offering. Giving is in response to one's faith, not their income level. It is making the work of Kingdom Building a priority.

In addition to working extremely diligently as Pastor of COD, there was my role as President of the national body of Black Clergy Women of the United Methodist Church. I was elected President in 2008 and we had a debt that was owed to the General Commission on Finance and Administration for $39,000. We paid the debt within two years through fundraising with the members of the group. We made an appeal each time that we met at Black Pastors, BMCR and Black Clergywomen. Our women were committed to the elimination of our debt because we wanted to maintain the good standings of our name.

After the debt was paid, we began to strategize for an annual meeting. We had meetings annually in different locations around the country, with the first being in Nashville, TN. Our Executive Leadership Team members, representative of all 5 Jurisdiction were, Dr. Jackie Rose Tucker, Vice President, Rev. Neriah Edwards, Clarifier, Rev. Marjorie Burns, Treasurer, Rev. Denise Picketts, Secretay, Rev. Candace Lewis, Chaplain, Rev. L. L. C. Hammond, Pastoral Care, Dr. Rosa Clements-Milner, Justice Coordinator and Ms. Stella Beene Venson, Meeting Planner. Our work would not have been as successful without the coordination of our Jurisdictional Coordinators.

During my leadership, we were so aware that we wanted to bring some of the best Preachers from Methodism and other denominations to share in our conferences. Rev. Candace Lewis accepted the role of coordination of the meetings, working closely with the Team. Our first meeting was held in Nashville, TN, and our final meeting under my administration was held in Dallas, Texas in 2013. During the Annual meeting we honored each of the previous Presidents, Bishop Linda Lee, Dr. Lydia Waters, Rev. Joyce Harris Scott, and Dr. Cynthia Belt.

> Bishops Violet Fisher, and Linda Lee,
> Rev. Jacqueline Waiters Lee and
> Dr. Alfreda Wiggins at 25th Anniversary Celebration

The first year, we brought Rev. Dr. Renita Weems, of the African Methodist Episcopal Church and seminary Professor, the nest year, we invited Rev. Dr. Gina Stewart, a Baptist Clergy Women from Tennessee, along with our strong supporters, Bishop Linda Lee, Bishop Violet Fisher and Rev. Dr. Gennifer Brooks, Garrett Evangelical Theological Seminary, Rev. Dr. Joy Moore, Associate Professor of Biblical Preaching, Luther Seminary.

The annual meeting of BCW required financial support and Dr. HiRho Park, of the General Board of Higher Education provided annual support to our group. Additionally, we raised funds from our various Annual Conferences, Colleges and Universities, the United Methodist Women, General Commission on the Status and Role of Women, Vendors, and through registration fees from the Clergywomen. Our goal and mission was to strengthen the skills and ministry of the Black Clergy Women around the nation. When I became President we were heavily in debt, however, at the close of my administration, we left more than $60,000 in the treasury.

Dr. Ouida Lee, Bishop Nhiwatiwa of Zimbabwe, Bishop Nahanala of Mozambique-, Bishop Linda Lee, USA and Dr. Kabamba Kiboka, African Clergywomen's President

At the invitation of Dr. Kabamba Koboko, I was invited to attend the African Clergy Women's Consultation. The day that I announced that I was going to attend the African Consultation, Bishop Fisher rose to share that I was their President and they wanted to support my expenses. She had me to stand and a glass was placed at my feet. She then asked the Clergy women to come forth and place money in the glass. BCW raised more than $1300 for my transportation cost. After I purchased my ticket, I received $1500 from GBHEM.

I was accompanied by my clergy sister, Rev. Dr. Martha Orphe of the Louisiana Conference. We flew to Johannesburg, South Africa and the

next evening we traveled by van into Harare. We were housed at the Holiday Inn in Harare and traveled to the campus each day. There were many women leaders from across the church who were present at the meeting. When we spoke, Dr. Koboko shared in conversation, some of the issues

Figure 1Dr. Hobson, Dr. Koboko, Bishop Lee, Dr. Martha Orphe, Dr. O Lee, Dr. HiRho Park

that faced the Clergywomen. It was my intent to respond to some of the concerns through my sermonic presentation. In conversation with the women, I learned that they served large churches, some of them 1500 members and above. In many ways their problems were similar to our own.

Those attending the Conference were from every African nation, therefore, the language barrier was a challenge. But the spirit of the conference was tremendous. It was a delight being with the women of Africa who sat with us and personally shared some of their struggles. The worship experience was a high and holy time and the women were open and listening as we participated with them. Lunch was served under a tent in order that we might all be together. And we met the first African Woman Bishop, Bishop Joaquina Filipe Nahanala from the Africa Central Conference and is appointed to the Mozambique Episcopal Area. It was a true blessing to represent the Black Clergy Women of the UMC. Wow!

Prayer was one of the essential ministries of our church. And I believe that Prayer held our congregation together and empowered us to rebuild as others left. We were a small group of about 8 people and we met each Saturday morning for prayer. We made a list of persons who requested prayer each week and distributed it to the membership on email. And on Saturday morning, we would gather in our prayer time and pray for each of them along with our personal concerns. On Sunday mornings, we would gather at the rear of the Sanctuary for Prayer with the Ushers. And during worship, we would gather each Sunday around the altar for Prayer. Our prayers were simple conversations with God about what was on our hearts. And we believed that we should pray without ceasing and that the Prayers of the righteous avails much.

In 2012, I was elected as a Jurisdictional delegate, which also serves as an Alternate delegate to the General Conference of the United Methodist Church, which was held in Tampa, Florida. This is a meeting of the church that brings people from every nation together to vote on changes to be adopted in the church. It was my first time attending and I was surprised at the variety of languages that were being spoken there and the methods of translation. The Conference was held in Florida and I shared a room with Rev. Deborah Chapman and she was a delightful travel companion. We were at the hotel with the Africa University Choir and they practiced in the Lobby every evening.

I had no idea about the expectations of the delegate, however, I made my way to every meeting that was required so that I could learn and represent well the people of the North Texas Conference. As a result of the time that we spent together, I felt prepared to step in when I was requested to do so. One of the major agenda items was the disbanding of some of the General Agencies of the United Methodist Church. One in particular was the General Commission on Religion and Race. There were many things that I did not understand, but I was confident that our Race problems had not been solved in the United Methodist Church. Originally the motion was passed on the floor, but after much discussion, it was decided that the action that had been taken was unconstitutional. The African American people who were in the stands were ecstatic about the reversal.

It is a strange place to stand when you are in the midst of people whose agenda is to go in one direction without consideration of those who are standing on the outside. One of the ways that policies get changed is through the democratic process of voting. I knew that I was concerned about the dismantling of some of the core agencies that has stood and attempted to assert justice in unjust actions. I could not with a clear conscious vote in support of the proposed actions. To think about those actions is to think about how it must have felt when after Emancipation Proclamation, Jim Crow Laws became the norm. Standing for Justice often finds the "justice seeker" standing on the outside. There is a sense that when we are truly open to justice, we are not quick to stand with "status quo." Simultaneously, one becomes aware that there are circles and covenant groups that you will not be invited into. One has to learn to accept that you may not be the "go along, to get along" person. If I believed that my actions only count right here, right now and that there are no ultimate consequential actions, perhaps I would join the crowd. But I believe there is a greater judge who calls and chooses persons to "speak truth to power" and simply "stand alone," while knowing that you are not alone.

The true Prophets that God called, as seen in the Biblical Scripture in Deborah, Elijah, Elisha, and yes even the women who made their way to the cross in the Gospel. All of them knew that they were called by God to make a stand and speak what God had given them to speak. It was not always accepted, but they spoke it out of their mouths, and God had and still has the final say so. So yes, when the Judicial Council ruled the actions taken by the General Conference unconstitutional, I was delighted. And even more so because one of the persons on the Council was a personal friend of mine.

We are not ready yet for the dismantling of the Commission of Religion and Race, but even if we do, that does not mean that we have truly become so open in the church that we will always take just actions. Justice does not mean a "free fall for all." What it does mean is that because of our "implicit bias, white privilege and supremacy," some will never have the opportunity to live out the fullness of their qualifications. God is still on the throne, and that is why, even in retirement, I continue to "press toward the mark for the prize of the high calling of God in Christ Jesus," Philippians 3:14.

When one lives on purpose, it would be easy to give up. I could have stayed at home and not gone to Florida. There were no funds within my local church budget for me to attend the General Conference, and we would be in a hotel for 12 days, add meals, transportation costs, and serving a small church. But I went, and bore all of the cost on my personal credit cards. Why? Because I had been entrusted and elected by the Conference, as the lone African American Clergywoman on the Team.

Life has to be lived on purpose. And I have come to understand that my purpose in life is to be an advocate for justice. It costs something to take a stand for justice, and for me that does not mean that I stand just for African Americans, but I stand for justice for all. There was a year in our Annual Conference when all of the Chairs of the Orders were all Anglo females. I raised the question on the floor of the Conference about the diversity of people in the Annual Conference and all that were elected were Anglo Females. The question was directed to the Bishop and it was casually dismissed. Later in the hallway between meetings the Bishop's Assistant shared with me "I named those women and there is nothing that you can do about it." I was later approached by a dear Clergywoman, the Reverend Kathleen Baskin Ball, (now deceased) who said, "Ouida, I can't do anything about the leaders of the Orders, but what I can do is, if you can get me the names of four persons I can appoint them to serve on the Board of Ordained Ministry." I named for her two African Americans, one male Deacon and one female Elder and one Hispanic Female Deacon and one Hispanic Male Elder. All of those persons were appointed. One has to have purpose in life and has to be willing to step forward to make a difference. I have made a conscientious decision to attempt to make a difference in this world, because I believe that our God will make the difference in the other. And there has to be those who are in the appointive authority with a sense of Justice and not merely White Privilege, or Racism."

In the year 2016 I was again elected to be a Jurisdictional Delegate, again serving as an alternate to General Conference. The Conference was held in Portland, Oregon. This was going to be the year of great change. We were again going to reorder the life of the Church. We were going to change the Book of Discipline of the Church to allow for the inclusion of LGBTQ people in full ordination rites within the church, or were going to cause a rift in the United Methodist Church. Although there had been much discussion about the issue and petition were prepared for the restructuring of the Church. And it appears that the line had been drawn in the sand. However, nothing was changed relative to Ordination and few issues were considered.

Prior to attending the General Conference, it is the work of the Delegation to be listeners and discerners to all groups. The ultra-conservative were preaching the wrath of God and had in many instances spoken with their congregation and had prepared them to leave the church. On the other hand, we listened to the more liberal voices as they spoke with compassion about the number of youth who were dealing with their sexuality and the numbers that were committing suicide. There was genuine concern raised by those who wanted to conduct the weddings of same-sex persons, especially after it became legal in the United States. Others were concerned about how it would be possible for a group so divided would have the potential to live together in Unity.

Many days we sat pensively in the huge auditorium and listened to the many debates, but we were always drawn back to reality by the margin of the votes that were taken. Simultaneously, the debates were interrupted by those who were agitating for change. We left Portland, Oregon without any change and with very little accomplished. However, within my own life, I have taken a stand for justice and have been fully aware that because of my stand, I have often had to stand alone. The reality is that I am not alone. Though you may not see my companion, but like the Hebrew boys thrown into the fiery furnace, I am accompanied by God the Father, His Son Jesus Christ and by the power of the Holy Spirit.

It was my feeble attempt to keep the congregation that I served aware of the issues before them. They never had any questions and neither did they share their thoughts. In many ways, after the thorough examination of the issues, I began to see the issue as a Justice Issue. I could recall the number of years that I had spent in the segregated Tatum Independent School District, where the Superintendent referred to us as the "Negra" school. The place where we never received new books, and even when the all-white School Board visited our school, they sat apart, in the center of the floor, while our parents sat in the bleachers. The school where our lunches came out of cans that had been provided by the US Military. Yet, we had the loving care of teachers, who sometimes were not adequately certified, but loved us enough to give us all that they had. Faculty that were committed to assuring us that we could become anything that we wanted to become. Faculty that were members of our local churches and knew our parents. Simultaneously, we were told that we were attending "separate but equal schools."

While I do not proclaim to have the perfect answer to the questions that still hold our Church in different camps, but I do believe that I know something about the God that we serve. The God of Abraham, Isaac and Jacob who has the capacity to see beyond all of our faults and sees our needs. The God who knew that "separate, but equal schools" were unjust.

Our God who saw our fathers and brothers die for a country that saw us as 3/5 of a person. The God who knew that one had to make courageous stands at the political booths, and eliminated the need to pay poll taxes in order to vote. We now see the efforts to suppress the vote by forcing voters to have "state issued identification," where some have to travel at least 125 miles to purchase the ID, while others can vote with their "gun permits." Our God is a great and awesome God who uplifts the downtrodden and humbles the haughty. There is a word recorded in Psalm 37:25, "I have been young, and now am old. Yet I have not seen the righteous forsaken, nor his descendants begging bread." And most of all, I am assured that as we draw closer to God, we have the opportunity to be changed by his compassionate ways. I have learned that I do not need to stand in the way of the Lord, nor make his judgements, God is well able to take care of each of his children.

Although I was not aware of it, my earliest existence was preparing me for the uncertainties of the future. Those words spoken so long ago in those classroom still reverberate in my consciousness, speaking confirmation and I believe that those "Ancestors" who lived through so many more hardships than I ever had to endure, empowered me to run on, there is a "great camp meeting on the other side." Their spoken words empowered me to pursue against the odds. Speak my truth. Strive to always give my best. Never worry about what others think. It does not even matter if you do not win the approval of man. Seek to honor God in all that you do, and know that you are on a journey called Life. The road is never straight, not always smooth, the curves are very deep and the hills are very high. But God will be your leveler in every situation.

After the 2016 General Conference, I was confirmed in my spirit that I would do all that I could to make a difference in the places that I was sent to serve, and that is never without a challenge. Still appointed at the Church of the Disciple, I would return and share with the congregation what had occurred, still no questions. Things had remained status quo and it appeared that all was happy.

During this time, I began to question myself about when I would retire. How does one know that it is time to retire? My health was very good and all was well with my soul and I still enjoyed the challenge of ministry. Ministry is not easy; but I loved the challenge of attempting to get the people of God to understand that God was with us, even in these difficult days. Money was still short and the summer was upon us. However, we had prepared ourselves to make it through the difficult summer season, by hosting our two annual events, Women's Day and Men's Day. We had put money in the Treasure to ensure us during the anticipated shortfall of the summer.

Upon my return from the Jurisdictional Conference, little did I know that I was preparing for my last four years in ministry? This was a time for transition. My mother, Mrs. Pearlie B. Isaac who had been such a determined figure in our lives while living at a Transitional Living Center in Longview had suffered another stroke. This time Mother was unable to communicate with us. She was begging for water, but when it was given to her, she would gag. Although the staff had effectively helped mother make it through so many of the difficult times, this time we took her to the hospital.

After arriving at Good Shepherd Hospital, along with her family. We attempted to cheer her through music which so often spoke to her soul. This time she did not react. Raising her hands and asking for water did not make a difference, because she could not swallow. She was placed on hospice and all of the family was summoned to be present with her. I shall always remember that walk as I followed her to the new part of the hospital. Tears were streaming down my face as we made our way to a new more comfortable location. Once in the Hospice Unit, Mother never said another word. We gathered. We sang. We prayed. No reaction. I spent the night in the room on Saturday and shared with the family that I was going home and would come back and stay with her.

I preached on that Sunday morning and had an engagement to preach on Sunday afternoon in Fort Worth. Between the services, I received a call that as my nephew entered the room to visit my mother on Sunday, she had already transitioned. My congregation wanted to know what I wanted to do. I responded that I was going ahead and preach. I did so. I believed that she wanted me to do so. Remembering David and how he prayed for his ill son, but when he died, he got up and moved on. In retrospect, I wondered if I had been in a state of shock. I was driven to the service in Ft. Worth by Keith Sharp, whom I fondly called my son. Accompanied by his wife Deborah. I was counseled by the Pastor of the Church who shared the loss of her mother. Yet, in my spirit, I felt that I had to keep going. Was I in denial? Shock? God held me close!

On Monday, I joined with my family in Longview as we prepared for the celebration of my Mother's life. We looked through old pictures, reminiscing about the past. Mother had been our center for such a long time. Especially since the death of our father in 1969, we had surrounded her with love and constant affection. She had worked for so many years into her eighties. My brother Jimmie had said it was time for her to retire. She was sort of a Matriarch at the Antioch Baptist Church, one of the oldest living members. She had been a member since youth along with her Mother, Mrs. Adeline Johnson who preceded her in death. Mother's celebration was held on a beautiful Saturday morning. The last of her eight siblings to die. Her nieces and nephews from all over were in attendance. They loved "Aunt Pearl." Many of the members of the Church of the Disciple, and Colleagues in Ministry from the North Texas Conference, Family and Friends from Dallas were present.

 I was the family spokesperson. I expressed thanks to the many family and friends, and especially to her niece Margie Centers, on whom she depended for explanation of things that she did not understand in life and for transportation to the hospital and doctor visits. I thanked her Church Family whom she loved and shared worship with over the years. I expressed thanks for the ways that she had always loved each of us as we grew up through life and the support that we all received. And I would have gone on for a while, but I heard the voice of my cousin Margie say, "That's enough," and I sat down. Mother had always been there for us, attending our graduations, and those of our children. She didn't miss much because she had her own personal driver, my sister, Sheila.

In July, I attended the Jurisdictional Conference of the United Methodist Church which was held in Wichita, Kansas. It should be noted that we have never elected an African American Clergywoman from our Jurisdiction. That year we had two African American Clergywomen, Rev. Dr. Janice Gilbert and rev. Cheryl Jefferson Bell, but neither one was elected. We also had the opportunity to make history by electing a Native American, Rev. David Wilson, Clergy of the Oklahoma Conference. However, the people made other choices. Change does not just happen, it takes persistence.

Ministry in the Church of the Disciple was somewhat waning, we felt the need for additional support of the Metro District Superintendent. With his support, a new program, "Healthy Church Initiative," was approved and undertaken. We had hopes that this program with the cooperation of all of the members would be a huge success. Clergy and Laity would study the same book with different leaders and would work together with a Coach to facilitate the program implementation. Monthly we would come together to discuss the books that we were required to read. A program was to be put together and presented to the church.

The Lay person who was the leader was expected to work with the Pastor and a presentation was to be made to the congregation. However, the leader of the Lay group put the program together and presented it to the Administrative Council before I saw it. During the course of the presentation, I asked a question about the implementation process and the leader became very defensive. These were questions that would have been asked prior to the presentation. However, when I attempted to discuss the matter with the lay person and the Coach, she put all of her material in a bag and said, "I quit." After making several attempts to work with the leader, the program had to be put on hold. She had developed all of the plans and others were not certain of what the next steps were. It is very difficult to work with persons who are unwilling to respect the leadership of the Pastor. Moreover, it is even more difficult to work with persons who have their own ideas because of prior leadership in other areas and believing that they have the final authority in matters that should be developed by a Team.

This was a great learning experience. The line of communication, though designed by the program, was not fully understood by the leader. Secondly, the Team concept of all working together to form the team; it should not have been a 'one person show'. Thirdly, respect and communication with the Pastor prior to presentation should have been clearly understood. Throughout the program that had been communicated that Lay and Clergy would meet separately for study, but should share their understanding of the study following each session. A great lesson from King Solomon as recorded in Scripture Proverbs 4:5-7, "Get wisdom, get understanding; forget it not; neither decline from the words of my mouth. Forsake her not, and she shall preserve thee" love her and she shall keep thee. Wisdom is the principal thing; therefore get wisdom; and with all thy getting get understanding."

The Mature Adult Ministry of COD celebrated its annual Platinum Plus Sunday. There always had to be Tea Cakes and punch served. I became the official Teacake baker. On the night before the bake-off, I would make up the batter, roll it for cutting and place it in the refrigerator. On the next day, several of the women of the ministry would gather to bake and wrap the cookies. Those were joyous times, lots of laughter and tasting. The Sunday would be the celebration with a creative program that had been developed by the Ministry. Our special choir would sing old gospel songs followed by a speaker. These were times of fellowship and celebration. It was a ministry of fellowship, celebration of birthdays, and holidays.

The month of August was a really special time with the Black Clergywomen of the United Methodist Church. We met annually in different cities across the United States for a time of study, praise and worship. The event was planned by the Executive Team of the group and would address current issues related to women in ministry. It was also very important that we would involve ourselves in a mission project within the Episcopal area that we were visiting. Although there are more than 700 Black Clergywomen across the nation, we often live in isolated areas. Therefore, when we came together, our celebrations were explosive worship experiences, with lots of laughter and fun between sessions.

We spent time in discernment about whether one of our clergy sisters was going to seek election to the Episcopal Office. It was very exciting to know that during the year 2016, we had four Black Clergy Women elected – Bishop Sharma Lewis, Bishop Tracy Smith Malone, Bishop Latrell Easterling and Bishop Cynthia Moore KoiKoi. They have joined ranks with Bishop Leontyne T. C. Kelly, Bishop Violet Fisher, Bishop Linda Lee and Bishop Beverly Shamana. These are women that we highly honor and support and appreciate their unique talents that honor, support, appreciate and strengthen the leadership of the Church. They are bold, courageous and loving leaders of the Kingdom of God. And they are strong supporters of the Black Clergywomen of the Church.

Our annual meetings have invited some of the premier Clergywomen across the world, Dr. Renita J. Weems, Rev. Dr. Carolyn Knight, Bishop Vashti Murphy McKenzie, Dr. Katie G. Cannon, Rev. Dr. Gina Stewart, whose giftedness has enhanced the life of the church and has empowered women in very special ways. As Clergywomen of the church, we are not concerned with doing things in traditional ways, rather, it is our intent to search the Scripture and with the power of the Holy Spirit, empower the people of God to live faithful lives that make a real difference in the world. And I am thankful to know that the Black Clergy women of the Church are standing tall and making a difference. Status quo is not good enough, God is calling us to reach beyond the breach and bring healing to our land.

In August 2016, the Clergywomen of the United Methodist Church met in Houston, Texas. All of the Women Bishops of the Church were present at this Quadrennial meeting and Clergywomen from around the world were present in Houston, Texas. It was a blessing to see such a great representation of Women Bishops and Clergy Women from around the world, together in sisterhood.

September of each year is a very special time for the women of the Status and Role of Women's Ministry of the Hamilton Park UMC. The location was the Hilton at Rockwall, TX. I was invited to be a speaker and to share an evening with them during their annual SROW Conference. In the midst of times that challenge us, God seemingly rewards us. The Rev. Dr. Janet Bell Odom was the Pastoral Host for this event. We shared a room and recalled many joyous memories and challenges of our work in the church. I recall reading a book that was written by Bishop Vashti McKenzie entitled, *"Journey to the Well."* She reminds the reader, through the story of the Samaritan Woman at the well, that there are times that we have one hope. From the Gospel of John Chapter 4, she had come for water, but left with living water. Her total life was changed when she met Jesus and was given a new agenda. Bishop McKenzie makes use of the woman having one last thing as she met Jesus at the well.

As Clergywomen, with the challenges that we face in life, we often find ourselves with one last thing in ministry as we attempt to assert ourselves to fulfill our duties to our God. Often we are challenged by the very people we are attempting to lead to a closer walk with Jesus. Unfortunately, many times, the women. Our Sisters who may be broken themselves, but are still stereotyping and holding women in the roles they believe that we should, or should not fill. Challenged by spouses who are unable to support us as we endeavor to lead the church. Sabotaged by those whose minds will not allow them to see us as the leaders that God has called us to be. At the well, Jesus invites us to take a sip of the living water and be made whole. I believe that Delores Williams adequately describes in her book, *Sisters in the Wilderness,* the experience that some African American women have experienced in ministry. Williams uses for an analogy, Hagar, who is fleeing Sari, "the wilderness experience means standing utterly alone, in the midst of serious trouble, with only God's support to rely upon[5]." It would be easy to give up, but there is a call from God and when one is called, one never gives up. We have been called to share a liberating word to the people of God. We have been called to stand on the wall and to execute with hands of justice. Will it always be accepted? No. But we stand anyhow.

We stand amid budgets that are too short and everyone is looking to you as the leader to bridge the financial gaps. I am thankful for my

experience in the Baptist Church where there is no agency that could possibly consider your plight and offer a helping hand. There is need for an entrepreneurial spirit for raising funds. Beautiful young teens had grown up in the church and were very talented. It occurred to me that we should ask their parents to allow their daughters to participate in a Debutante for Christ pageant. Each young lady would have a sponsor would fundraise by soliciting ads for a souvenir booklet. The event would feature each teenager sharing a talent, singing, liturgical dance, spoken word, or musical instruments. They would be escorted by their fathers and share a faith statement. Finally, each would receive a participant award and the one with the highest financial total would be crowned. Each of the girls were beautifully dressed in white gowns and there was a team of

---

[5] Williams, Delores S. Sisters in the Wilderness – The Challenge of Womanist God-Talk. P. 109. Orbis Books. New York. 1994.

outside judges to judge their talents. The atmosphere was ecstatic and was well attended by the community. The event raised more than $10,000 even at the time of a critical financial crisis. Maya Townsend, Kennedy Lusk, Taylor Dunn, Devin Holloway were participants and Sydney Sharp was crowned the winner.

The Church of the Disciple tried many strategies to become known throughout the community. One of them was to have our Bible Study at a community restaurant. Our first stop was Wing Stop. We ordered and shared with each other as we shared a meal at a back table. As others came in, we invited them to come and share with us in study. The Prayer Team shared a Saturday morning Prayer Session on the patio at Starbucks. We had learned that Church could happen anywhere and were putting it into practice.

My heart was always focused on the members of the congregation, especially when they experienced loss, or significant celebrations. With friends, we traveled to Arkansas, to Galveston, and Louisiana, and within Texas to Sherman and Denison. I did it all in support of their families, but when it came my time, the support was not always returned. These experiences taught me that it is only what you do for Christ that will last. And when you give of yourself, God sends blessings and favor in your life. This is a promise from God, "Give, and it will be given to you. Good measure, pressed down, shaken together, running over, will be put into your lap. For with the measure you use it will be measured back to you," Luke 6:38 (ESV). There are times that we think of this verse when we are expecting monetary gifts, but hear these words, "Do not be deceived, God is not mocked; for whatever one sows, that will he also reap.," Galatians 6:7 (ESV). There is true freedom in the word of the Lord.

Each December was a very special time of the year. It was the ending of one year and my intentions were to prepare for a brand new beginning. There were always those end of the year statistical reports, and preparing them this year was no different. The one constant thing was my personal report of my journey for the year, the courses that I had taken, the places that I had been to and engaged in ministry. I was fully confirmed in my spirit that I had early morning devotions daily and that I prayed personally and with the Prayer Ministry. As I reflected back over the year, even the daunting task of ministry could not deter my spiritual energy. I walked alongside of those who lost loved ones, prayed and visited those who were hospitalized. And yes, I had been challenged when I lost my own mother this year. Our financial status had not changed. However, by faith, we paid all of our indebtedness. God is good all of the time.

The Mayflower High School graduation class of 1967 were planning a celebration for our 50th year Reunion. We were a class of 28 graduates,

but we made plans for a grand celebration. We gathered at the home of the Hightowers for our first planning meeting. The event was held at the Tatum High School in November. There was no speakers, but a huge celebration. Although many of us had moved away, we wanted to honor the hometown leaders of Tatum who had made significant contributions to the quality of life in Tatum. The event was a huge success. Wow! We talked and danced the night away. (Pictured are Alton Ramsour, Mercy Bradford, Christine Peterson, Ouida Isaac, Charles Hightower, Carolyn Centers, and Jessie Sammons – Maiden names).

Christmas was also a very special time for the Platinum Plus Ministry. It was our time to go to the Thorntree Country Club for our special time of sharing gift exchange. The senior adult ministry of the church really loved this time of the year, a buffet luncheon and numbers drawn from a bag would allow each of us to receive the numbered gift. Fellowship was shared by each of the women as we chatted among ourselves. Acts 2:42 give us an example of the expectation that the Christian community should live, "They devoted themselves to the apostles' teaching and fellowship, to the breaking of bread and the prayers." (NRSV). And in the words of one of my favorite Gospel, "What a fellowship, what a joy divine, leaning on the everlasting arms."

Christmas was a special time in our ministry. We hung the holly and decorated the church. Families were asked to light the Advent Candle each Sunday. We were being ushered into the New Year. Believing that I still had the energy to lead the Church into the future, we set our eyes on new beginnings. And the Platinum Plus Ministry always attempted to reach out to our seniors who were shut-ins. As the designated driver of the

Church van, I drove the group to visit, shared the Christmas story, sang and prayed. Each shut-in received a gift basket.

There had been a constant question in my mind, as to when would I retire. I thought perhaps 2017, but that was an odd number year. Maybe 2018 would be the year. I'm just not certain. I love the Pastoral Ministry, even its challenges. Once the year begins, it seems to move quickly, especially for a Pastor who had been involved not only in the local church, but in the Conference, the Jurisdiction, and national matters. There is the role of facilitating the preparation of an Elder for Ordination, attending with the youth Confirmation, local Black Methodist for Church Renewal, General Black Methodist for Church Renewal and Fundraising for Africa University.

I accepted an assignment with the national body of "Strengthening the Black Church for the 21st Century" within the Southwest Texas Conference. Two Pastors were assigned to me, one who served a two point charge, Dale Corinth, near Austin, TX and the other was located in Kerrville, TX. I made visits to each of these churches in order to meet with their Pastor and Administrative Staff. My intent was so that we might set goals and work toward attaining them. This assignment required monthly calls and bi-annual visits. My role with these churches was to serve as a Coach. Our training was done through the General Board of Discipleship in Nashville, TN. Our Team of Coaches were invited to Austin, TX to conduct a seminar for the Pastors of the SWTX Conference. The premise of Coaching is that the vision of the individual being coached lies within. It is goal of the Coach to help crystalize and bring to fruition the vision.

The year is flying by and I had been invited by a friend to visit Los Angeles, CA. Rev. Adrienne Zackery welcomed me into her beautiful home. And the real purpose for my visit was so that we could hit the shopping district. There are stores in the District that meet whatever your taste, from casual to suits of all types. And there are shoes by all designers. We could have spent days there. There were special lunches and late dinners. And the special day that we spent in the Glen Ivy Spa at the foot of the mountains. And yes, I had a few hours to spend with my high school classmate, Felma Jackson. In the midst of times that are challenging, it is good to know that it is possible to share time with friends. Scripture reminds us, "A friend loves at all times," Proverbs 17:17. (NIV)

Education has always been so important to me, I suppose that is why I did it so many times. Therefore, graduations were very special times in the life of our church. I would don my doctoral cap and gown and would ask the students to wear their graduation gown. Our Minister of Music, Regina Lee would play "Pomp and Circumstance" for our entry into worship. Even though our funds were limited, I insisted that each student who was attending college would receive a letter announcing their $500 Scholarship, along with a certificate from the church. When the student registered for college, we would send half of the scholarship. The other half would be sent when the student registered for the next semester. Additionally, the General Board of Higher Education and Ministry would offer scholarship dollars to each United Methodist student who attended college, if a letter of support was written by the Pastor. With love for each of the students who graduated, I attended their parties and made personal contributions to each student. I am encouraged by the words of I John 4:8, "He who does not love does not know God, for God is love." (NKJV).

The church finances were very short which meant that we would not have the money to make it through the tough summer months. I suggested to the Finance Committee that we should have a Revival. If they were in agreement, I would invite three preachers and inform them of our financial status and would ask them to preach one night each. I would offer to come and preach for them at any time as our form of repayment. I contacted three of my friends, the Reverend Oscar Epps of the Community Missionary Baptist Church, the Reverend Todd Atkins of the Salem Institutional Baptist Church and the Reverend Ritchie Butler of the St. Paul United Methodist Church. Rev. Epps shared that this was his vacation season and that he had promised his wife that he would not take another preaching engagement. However, he would send one of the preachers of his church and he would pay the preacher and send us an offering. I was so grateful.

The Reverend Alene Denson arrived from the Community Missionary Baptist Church and was accompanied by their dynamic Women's Choir and preached the congregation into a frenzy. The Rev. Todd Atkins, my husband's Pastor accepted and he was accompanied by the Salem Congregation. The Rev. Ritchie Butler also accepted our invitation and shared a powerful word. The Finance Committee asked each member to donate $100 for the Revival and the congregation agreed. Although this was a financial fund raiser, the congregation was inspired and motivated by the Word of the Lord that was preached each evening. I will always remember the words of several of the members, "We are so sorry that this Revival is over, we so enjoyed it." I am reminded of the words of a song written by Byron Cage, "Oh how good it is to be in the presence of the Lord, my soul rejoices in the presence of the King. Makes me want to sing, makes me shout, makes me want to holler, throw up my hands!" Worship. And the experience of having the support of friends is invaluable. It is indeed a blessing to have the support of those who love the Lord and are willing to extend a helping hand to a colleague in ministry who is experiencing difficulties.

The very next day at the Hamilton Park United Methodist Church, we celebrated the 75th Anniversary of Mr. & Mrs. Curtis Smith. This loving couple had surrounded me during my three year tenure at their church. I could not miss their celebration because my mind was filled with the memories of breakfasts and lunches at their home. And infamous visits to the farm to fish and share with their family. Precious memories of love that we shared. And Mrs. Smith made the best homemade cakes and pies.

Back in the great City of DeSoto, the Honorable Mayor Curtistene McCowan and Councilmembers along with the citizens honored the Police Department, led by Chief Joseph Costa. Concerned Pastors in small town communities are totally immersed in its activities. I was there onsite to offer prayer for the group as we gathered. And of course when Chief Costa became Chief, we invited him to share with our Church in the worship service. The statistics of the Police Department shared during our monthly meetings of DeSoto Police and Clergy (DPAC), revealed that our highest crime within the city was Domestic Violence. Therefore, the Police Headquarters became the location of the monthly meeting of the Domestic Violence Advisory Commission (DVAC). It should not be a surprise that when the first Symposium of DVAC was held at the Church of the Disciple. We were honored to host more than 700 persons, including the High School ROTC members, community residents and survivors in our sanctuary and classrooms.

Church Anniversaries were very special times and in the year 2017, the Soror Rev. Cokeisha Bailey Robinson was our honored guest. A true time of celebration for our congregation and to hear the word of the Lord from a dedicated woman of God. We were nearing the end of the church year and again finances were always a major part of the celebration. It was never our intent to be the congregation that would make numerous requests, we simply shared our expectations and accepted whatever the membership placed on the table…we were rarely disappointed.

A church in the community and always concerned about the safety of the children, we hosted a safe alternative to Halloween. Ministries of the church decorated rooms and invited the community in to share in the festivities. Always, the guest left with invitations to come back and share worship with us.

After the death of my mother, my sister Sheila, the baby of the family became the person who attempted to keep the family together for celebration. And Thanksgiving was one of those special occasions. The family gathered at my brother Elnoris' house. We took lots of Family pictures because things had changed since our last gathering here…mother was gone.

50 Year High School Reunion

Only a couple of days later, the Class of 1967 was going to celebrate our 50th Reunion. We had button that everyone received and their names were printed on them. We had prepared souvenir booklets to be shared with every attendee. Every student of class of 67 received a T-shirt and we had others for sale. There were pins that recognized that we were the last class to graduate from the Mayflower (Colored/Negra) School. And our most prized gift to the class were special commemorative pins representing our 50th year. And we had special pins that were given to Margie Centers, Retired Assistant to the Superintendent, and Mr. Nelson Representative of the Town, along with Mr. Drennon Fite, first Black Trustee of the Board of Education. We closed it down, but we were there to commemorate it. Carolyn Price and I made our way to Tatum early so that we could decorate and set things up. As we were attempting to contact members of the 1967 Class, we found a member whom none of us had heard from for 50 year, Lee Cass Price. We were all so happy to see him and he and Carolyn danced the night away. And I should not forget that our Class President, Charles Hightower served as the Master of Ceremonies. And my daughter, Regina Lee, became the star of the show when she sang a specially worded song to the tune of "At Last." This was such a fun filled evening and perfect in every way, so much that I will live longer because of it. Psalm 133:1. "How very good and pleasant it is when kindred lived together in unity!"(NRSV).

Looking great after 50 years and what a celebration – Wow!!

My last book was entitled, *Simply Pray*. The intent of the book was to share with other how easy it is to pray. I believe that we do not need to establish a ritualistic prayer, repeating words that you have heard others say. Rather, I believe that the Lord wants to hear the desires of our hearts individually. Our concerns, our hurts, disappointments, joy and celebrations. Our God is big enough to know, hear and is concerned about whatever concerns us. And as a result of the book, I was invited to submit my book by for review and in competition with other authors. I was honored to have been considered by the Christian Literary Guild. I invited family and friends to surround me for the event. Although I did not win, it was an honor to have been considered.

Christmas had come so soon. There was shopping, and cooking to be done and the wrapping of gifts. It is always a joy for me to shop for the family and attempt to get everyone something that I thought they will enjoy. Christmas dinner was at the Parsonage. The entire counter is filled with good things to eat and we settle in for a time of gift opening and sharing a meal. I loved shopping for my family. And I always loved shopping for the children of my niece Shesheika, a beautiful and committed mother. My sister would share, whatever you purchased for Christmas would be their attire on the first Sunday in the New Year. And there were friends, those who had been particularly supportive of me during the year, I would not dare forget them at this special time. There were special cakes and pies to be baked and the delight of preparing a meal for my family, something that I could not do on a weekly basis because of Church obligations. Each Christmas, we would stay around the counter and hold hands and give thanks to God for all of the blessings of family. For me it was so important to make memories, time was moving on and family was growing smaller.

It is amazing to me how time brings about a change in life. One day while shopping in the local Albertsons' I met with a memory from the past. It was a former member who stopped to speak with me. He shared that his wife had died and that he was about to be married again. He invited me to attend his wedding. I was honored. Several weeks later at the wedding, there were so many of the former members of the Church in attendance. I arrived a bit late because I got lost. When I arrived, the wedding party was forming a reception line. I was greeted by the Bride and Groom at the door, along with several other former members. There were questions about how the church was doing, to which I responded, "God is holding us in the palms of his hands." Through the many difficulties in Ministry, God had taught me that if I ministered in love, all would be well. I was present with a gift for the newlywed couple.

Saturday mornings was the time that the Prayer Ministry met. We did not simply pray for those of us who were in attendance, but we prayed for the Church, its ministries and the members of the congregation. We were a group that believed in interceding on behalf of others, therefore, our prayers also included the concerns that we had for others in our families, community and the world. The group was committed and were foundational for the success of the work of the church.

I served as one of the founding members of the African American Pastors' Coalition. This was the first Interdenominational group of Pastors in Dallas and the Metro Area that allowed women to be recognized and to be contributing members of the group. Our annual celebration was held on Martin Luther King's birthday each year. The entire city would be invited to attend and share in worship at one of our larger congregations. Several years I served as Secretary and was then nominated to be Vice President of Communication. It was an honor to serve along with Rev. Zan Holmes, the late Dr. E.K. Bailey, Rev. Dr. Frederick D. Haynes, III, Rev. Dr. Jerry

Christian, Rev. Bryant Carter, Rev. Dr. David Henderson, the late Rev. John C. Morris, Jr., and Rev. Delphine Vasser as Officers.

There were many other Pastors who served as members of the AAPC and we believed that we were called to make a difference in our Dallas Community. In addition to our MLK Celebrations, we often coalesced concerning issues of race and police brutality. Leaders are called to stand on the forefront of issues within our communities. Ezekiel 33:6 reminds us, "But if the watchman sees the sword coming and does not blow the trumpet, so that the people are not warned, and the sword comes and takes any one of them, that person is taken away in his iniquity, but his blood I will require at the watchman's hand."

The experience of ministry taught me that Church truly could happen anywhere. It could have been sharing lunch with the Platinum Plus

Ministry, or entertaining the community in ministry with the Eggstravaganza. Or, fellowshipping with my African American sisters and brothers in our General meeting of Black Methodist for Church Renewal in many cities across the United States. And it is always church when the women come together in celebration of Annual Women's Day. Or, perhaps celebrating with the local elected officials as City Boards and Commissions were

recognized. And sometimes traveling to the State Capitol in Austin, TX to open the State House of Representatives at the invitation of the Honorable State Representative Yvonne Davis. And upon your arrival realizing that there is a special parking place for the Pastor of the Day. And maybe just maybe you would be honored to act as Principal of the Day for your local School District. And there is a time of celebrating great friends, honoring the life and legacy of my friend Mrs. Mollie Stewart, a dynamic Laywoman of the Southeast Jurisdiction of the United Methodist Church. And a leader in the General Church and many of its agencies,

especially the Hinton Center and Gulfside Assembly. Community engagement makes a difference.

The role of the Pastor is to be a community leader. That is why, it was important to me to give of the best that I had to the community. It was not for my name to be called, but rather for the Church of our God would be represented in all arenas of life. Yes, I went to birthday parties, bridal showers, baptized new Christians, attended funerals and celebrated with the high school in parades. And when the community called, I was there to pray. Because we serve a God who invites us to share the love of Jesus Christ wherever we go. Yes, there is written in the book of Ecclesiastes chapter 3,

"There is a time for everything, and a season for every activity under the heavens....a time to mourn and a time to dance."

It was in November of 2018 that my husband of 46 years John C. Lee, Jr died. He remained a stalwart member of the Salem Institutional Baptist Church all of his life. And his dedicated service to the U.S. Postal Service spanned more than 50 years. A committed and dedicated Deacon, who loved Baptist Training Union and

served as its Director for many years, Sunday School Teacher to Youth and Adults, and sang for many years in the Senior Choir. He slept quietly away in the early morning of November 14th. He fought the good fight of faith and finished his course in a whisper, yet he made a difference in our lives and his place will never be filled. His memory lives on in our heart. Having faced death in so many ways, I learned that, "He will wipe every tear from their eyes." Revelation 21:4 (NIV).

My husband was ill while I was attempting to complete my last year of Pastoral Ministry. It was a difficult journey because he was now almost completely on a walker. I am so thankful for my friend Nurse Deborah and her husband Keith who enabled me in so many ways to complete my final year. Nothing was beneath them to do in order that I might succeed. These were challenging days at church, and also at home. I recalled the word of

Scripture which reminds us from the book of Romans 8:28, "All things work together for the good of them who loved the Lord and are called according to his purpose." May I share that even though it is working for our good, it does not always feel good. We are called to TRUST God.

Then there was Thanksgiving. My loving Sister wanted the Family to gather for Thanksgiving and family had come from all around Texas to share in this very special time of giving thanks. There we were right in the midst of funeral and now we were moving to festival. I was not certain how I felt, this was not a time of great celebration, although we had celebrated at the funeral. And now life has changed in many ways, in many ways, it had changed forever. Though I could have long conversations and complaints about the things that I was not pleased with. It is over. I was on my own to make decisions and choices. However, as in times past, I heard the gentle reminder from God, "Be still and know that I am God." And my solid promise, "I will never leave you, nor forsake you." I am not alone. God is with me.

I had shared with the congregation that I would be retiring in June of 2019. I recall attending the retirement celebration of several members of the Salem Church earlier in my ministry. And I wanted my celebration to be on that scale. Fully aware that our church could not afford to pay for the event, I organized a Team from inside and outside of the church to help me plan. The Team was made up of several members of the Staff Parish Relations Committee and community members. A great vision was cast and the Team was ready to make it become a reality. We sold tickets in order to pay for the event and there were donations made by some members of the Team.

It was a celebration that made my heart happy. The event was held at the Double Tree by Hilton Hotel Campbell Centre on Saturday April 27 at 12 Noon. The decorations were unbelievable. The music was awesome. My speakers shared my story. All of my immediate family were present. And friends were there from California, Chicago, and Arkansas. It was the celebration of my 50 years in Ministry, including 28 years in Pastoral Ministry along with my Lay Leadership, and my 70th birthday. I was bedazzled in a Red Suit representative of my Delta Sisterhood. And the Rev. Dr. Zan W. Holmes, Jr. who accepted me in Pastoral Ministry at the St. Luke Church in the beginning, was there to say a message for my retirement.

This was a proud but humble moment for me in Ministry. The entry way to the celebration area was a red and white balloon arch developed by Mrs. Charlene Hampton. I entered the event to the tune of Sophisticated Lady and had so many words of thank you for those who were present. My photographer, Mrs. Sylvia Dunnavant Hines came and took photos and gave me a book of memories. The souvenir booklet was developed and printed by Mrs. Pat Wilson. The beautiful and tasty cake was done by Carolyn Hill. And the beautiful candy bar was donated by Mrs. Toni Allen. I thank God for friends. Friends who were willing to support my celebration and to come and share words of expression and love at a time that my life was taking a new turn. I am thankful to God who has led me on this journey of life and allowed me to see the highs and the lows. I never consider myself to be very savvy, but it has always been my intent to go on the journey to see where it would lead me.

In the afternoon, the Sunday following my retirement celebration the word of the Lord was preached powerfully by my friend, the Reverend Wanda Bolton Davis, and oh what a word. She reminded me that though I was retiring, my work was not finished. My friends and colleagues were present: District Superintendent Debra Hobbs Mason, former Senior Pastors with whom I served, Dr. Ron Henderson, Rev. Tyrone Gordon and so many other colleagues. And the most humbling of all was the prayer that was prayed for me as I was surrounded by my colleagues. Wow, what a ride!!

After the celebration, I found myself really looking forward to retirement. Throughout my life, I had been so busy doing, I was quite unsure of what it would feel like to be still. I would work through the month of May, because by now the new Associate Pastor was leading the church. There was so much in my office to pack, after all in twelve years one accumulates so many mementos and treasured gifts. The desktop alone was covered with so many pictures of the students who had graduated high school and some even college. There were treasured items that I had picked up around the world, a silver challis and plate that I picked up in Jerusalem, purchased with funds from Mrs. Eartha Pitts Mitchell. A miniature of my dream car donated by Deborah Sharp. A large picture that hung in front of my desk donated by the United Methodist Men under the leadership of Bernard Brown. A beautiful statue that stood over my shoulder donated by Dr. Shelia Brown. Angels donated by more friends than I can remember and figurines of dogs donated by my friend Wendy Lee, the dog rescuer. There was a Crystal Cross paper clip holder given to me as a gift for a wedding that I performed, and one from the Hamilton Park UMC, and a gold plated clock donated by the Sherman Ministerial Alliance. And I should mention the accommodations shared from Mayor Curtistene McCowan. And my office was filled with love, surrounded by my family with special portraits of my family. Such precious memories and the love that was shared with me over the years. The desk was filled with special cards that had been shared with me on birthdays and holidays, filled with timeless notes, special memories. I should mention the many bibles, commentaries, and books that supported the ministry and my theological position.

The last day of my Pastorate, I preached the morning worship. It was a sad time for me, I had loved my work at the Church of the Disciple. The

Office of the Pastor is finally clear of all of the things that I treasured. It is now open for whoever will occupy it next. The choir would sing for the very last time in my presence. The Ushers at the door were greeting me for the last time as Pastor. The children and the Youth whom I had nurtured were present and my Senior Adults were there. I missed two families that had been prominent during my tenure there, Lon and Gloria Cardwell who had been so welcoming and never left me, though their health was failing. Earlier in 2019 we had celebrated the life of Lon, but his faithful

Gloria was still there. And there was Michael Matthews who told me that he would never leave. A faithful Usher who greeted me every Sunday until his health failed him. His life too had been celebrated earlier that same year.

I had attended Sunday School that final Sunday with My Class, where Brother Preston Crenshaw was the teacher. They were all there Ms. Alice Price, Mrs. Shirley Isaac, Mrs. Jeanette Mulaula, and Dr. Vickie Smith. For the life of me, I do not recall the title or text of my final sermon. The keys were ready to be turned over to the Chair of Trustees, Doris Burke. But there is one more service – my final afternoon. There were so many memories and people who had passed through the doors. In thirteen years there were those who came and united with us and there were those who simply came and went. There were those who were supporters who gave their very best in service, and other who sat on the sideline. It was my goal to preach the Gospel message in ways that we could encounter Jesus within the story and within our lives. And I had a great love for teaching the children the great stories of the Bible. I wanted them to come to know that even though you may not see in physical manifestation our Savior, but that God is always near. It is my personal belief that our God comes near to us in our journey through life and at no time are we completely alone when we put our whole trust in God.

My friends, I recall reading in the word of the Lord as recorded in the Gospel of John, chapter 20 verses 30-31, "Jesus performed many other signs in the presence of his disciples, which are not recorded in this book. But these are written that you may believe that Jesus is the Messiah, the Son of God, and that by believing you may have life in his name." These verses help me because there is so much more that I could share with you and even some that I dare not pen, the dark places, times that I got lost, but not from God. Thank you Jesus. I have come to know that in spite of the things that I did, I learned from God's Word, "If we claim to be without sin, we deceive ourselves and the truth is not in us. If we confess our sins he is faithful and just and will forgive us our sins and purify us from all unrighteousness." I John 1:9 (NIV). These verses I learned early in life and came to understand that on my journey, I was not at all perfect, but I was forgiven. They freed me to live my life for Christ and to do his will and not be weighed down by unnecessary baggage. For those who would have a life of such purity that you have committed no sin and find it difficult to believe that it is possible for sinful people to be forgiven, I direct you to Isaiah 55:8-9. "For my thoughts are not your thoughts, neither are your ways my ways, declares the Lord. As the heavens are higher than the earth, so are my ways higher than your ways and my thoughts than your thoughts." (NIV). Thank you God for your grace and mercy, allow each of us to look into the mirror of our own souls.

June 30, 2019 has finally arrived. There is no real fanfare. Jesus is the guest of the hour. I preached my final sermon to the congregation. I do not recall the text, nor the title of the last sermon. What I do recall is that as I stood at the back door for the last time, I passed the keys on to Trustee Chair, Mrs. Doris Burke. I stood by my car and asked that this picture be taken as I waved goodbye.

July 2019 began a new chapter in my life, it was called 'Retirement.' But what am I do with all of this time that I have on my hands? Household chores have never been my favorite thing to do. And though I love to travel, that takes real money. Church is now a whole new arena with questions, where do I serve? Will I be welcomed? What will I do in ministry?

The first few months I was preaching at different churches. It was joyful. My mind was completely clear, no budgetary concerns, or attendance worries, or even if the music coincided with my sermon. I was free to simply preach and go home, no Church Council, or Staff Pastor Parish Relations Committee. And through most of the years of my life, there was not time for watching television, I could now watch as much as I wanted to. And with Netflix, I could watch a whole series uninterrupted. I could contemplate the actions and almost figure out the endings and who the real criminals were. I was a Pastor and thought I would make a commitment to the Salem Institutional Baptist Church. This is the Church that had limited my participation and refused to allow me to live out my call to ministry. That was in 1991, twenty eight years ago. There is a younger Pastor who invited me to share with him in ministry. I was invited to lead Bible Study, preach and lead an online Prayer Ministry.

Did I mention that I like to travel? There had been a cruise to Mexico in July and my retirement trip to Australia, inclusive of a 10 day cruise in October. In the meantime, I decided to explore Hospital Chaplaincy. Methodist Charlton accepted me as an Intern. This was a short-term responsibility, October through February. Ministry in this arena was quite different from Pastoral Ministry, although I found a great love through my encounters with patients. And yes, I learned more about myself and ways of handling general life situations through the critical work done with patients. Another graduation and retirement occurred in February, and though I had purposed in my mind that I would

return to do Residency with the hospital I was not accepted. I was told that there were only 5 positions. This is it, my Final Retirement.

I had always wanted to write my life story and I began the task of telling my story of the many ways that I have seen God intervene in my life. This is it. I am now 71 years old and had plans to take a few of my friends on a fishing trip in March, but the deadly Corona virus became more pervasive and we postponed the trip. We are forced to shelter in place and practice social distancing and constant washing of our hands. For the first two months, I hardly left my house. I undertook a new task, the yard. My husband had been unable to upkeep due to his health, and it is now my responsibility to do so. Cutting it was not enough. The lawn man only mowed and edged, but I wanted to pull the weeds as I had seen my husband do so often. One day in the midst of my sitting on the ground, I pulled a weed and saw a head pop through the ground. It was a snake! The neighbor across the street saw me hop up and asked what was wrong? I said, "It is a snake." He came over and pulled him into the street. But the joke among all of my friends was, a snake of any size is an "Anaconda."

I shared earlier that I had only one sister, Sheila and she wanted all of us to gather at her house during the Memorial Holiday. We all lived in big cities and Covid 19 was running rampart. I kept telling her to stay at home and not go to church, but she was insistent that COVID19 was only the flu. I told her it was so much more serious and that she needed to stay home. She was already suffering with Congestive Heart Failure and had a persistent cough. One of her members insisted that she should go and get checked because several members had already tested positive, and when tested they confirmed Covid19 and pneumonia. She had to be hospitalized, but was released after three days. I could not believe that she had made such a speedy recovery with her heart condition. I was so excited when she was sent home. During the course of the two weeks that she had been sheltering in place, we spoke often. She was such a powerful Prayer Warrior and since I had the Thursday Night Prayer Call at Salem, I asked her to pray. She told me that she did not feel like praying and I accepted that.

I called her late on Saturday night, because I knew she was always up late at night. We shared a conversation about the fact that my brother had mowed her lawn and found a $100 bill that was turning brown on her lawn. We shared laughter in our usual sisterly talks. And on Sunday afternoon my brother Jimmie, who lives in Katy called and asked, "Ouida did you know that Sheila died?" I was driving and screamed "what Sheila?" He responded "our sister." Even as I type this part of the story, tears are welling up in my eyes. This is the same brother who called me when my Father died. And with the same soft voice. I was riding with my friend Deborah and she asked me to pull over so that she could drive. I would not, I told her I was in control of the vehicle. I drove home as I cried aloud and called my daughters. Regina first no answer. Then Libbie. Shanel. While driving home I cried aloud. As soon as I arrived home, people began to come in. I called Pastor Todd Atkins and he called the women whom he knew I was close to, Mrs. Mable Levine and Ms. Shirley Wheeler, and they arrived shortly after I got home.

I wanted to leave immediately because my sister had only one child and I wanted to be with her. I could only imagine how she must have felt. This was the day that she had come out of quarantine and could have visitors. She did not die in the hospital alone, but in her home alone. I needed to get there. And I did, Angie, my Cousin who has been like a daughter to me showed up and she drove me to my niece that night. We met two days later to make plans for her celebration of life. It had to be outside, under a tent and her gravesite is separated from Daddy and Mama, by one grave, but is next to our paternal great grandmother. Since her burial, the song that I have played over and over is, I'm Really Going to Miss You as sang by Smokey Robinson. Again I am reminded of the words of Scripture, I

Corinthians 15:51-55 (NIV) and comes as an announcement, "Listen, I tell you a mystery: we will not all sleep, but we will all be changed – in a flash, in the twinkling of an eye, at the last trumpet. For the trumpet will sound, the dead will be raised imperishable, and we will be changed. For the perishable must clothe itself with imperishable, and the mortal with immortality. When the perishable has been clothed with the imperishable, and the mortal with immortality, then the saying that is written will come true: Death has been swallowed up in victory. Where, O death, is your victory? Where, O death, is your sting?" Death does not have the final word.

After such a tragic loss, I have attempted to consume myself with life giving things, flowers and vegetables. I had always loved flowers and wanted to plant some for curb appeal. I planted beautiful plants and took their pictures and posted to Facebook. As they grew and blossomed, I was very proud of them watering them daily, weeding them as necessary. I am even spending time learning from the internet how to grow special plants. I learned from my brother that there are certain vegetables that have to be planted at certain times if they are to produce, specifically greens, beans, cucumbers and squash. I will be prepared for the next season.

The lawn man noticed a plant that I was unfamiliar with and shaped it up. I started to water it and now it is so beautifully covered with flowers. And in the flower bed out back there are the cannas. I had never really paid attention to them. I was too busy living…new life, new learnings. But I saw them pictured on a friend's Facebook page and decided to water them and to do a bit of research. The first one is blooming and the whole bed of them have taken on new life. I learned that they need lots of water to produce. Water is life giving to plants, like the water of the word brings new life to people. Jesus said that in John chapter 4:12-14 (NIV), "Everyone who drinks this water will be thirsty again, but whoever drinks the water I give them will never thirst. Indeed, the water I give them will become in them a spring of water welling up to eternal life." I only wish it worked like that for plants, but I am sure that it works in the lives of humanity.

None of life is without its challenges, but as I listened to a message preached by Bishop T. D. Jakes, as he discussed the scraps that the Disciples picked up after the feeding of the five thousand men, not including the women and children. The Scraps are a reminder of what God has already done in our lives and that wherever we go, God is with us. The leftovers are there as a reminder that whatever miracle God has performed that God is still the same God between our miracles. It is when the storms come that we sometimes forget what God has done. Thank you God for your confirming word in my life as recorded in Psalm 46:10........Be still and know that I am God.

I am thankful for this journey that I have been on, although there are times that it has been so difficult. But because I TRUST God, even in the difficulties, I have learned to forge my way on in faith. Is that easy? No, but it pays to know that all things are working for my good, even when I want things to happen right now, I trust God to know that God has a plan for my life. And a statement that I have used repeatedly, "Life is a mystery to be lived and not a problem to be solved." The result of ultimate trust in God is a renewing of your faith. We have the leftovers in our minds and remember the last time that God has worked things out on our behalf and because we TRUST God, we believe that it will happen again...It is called faith.

Faith grows through challenging times. And yes, we are being challenged in many ways with the Covid19 virus, and black men and women who continue to die through Police brutality. And I should not fail to mention the "charged" political environment and the threat of the Voters Right Act. And the continuous challenge of people of color who are threatened on every hand and we simply want to live our lives in peace with all. But faith makes one more tolerant of the issues of life, especially those things that you have no control over. This statement may be difficult for the mind that has not come to believe in the power of God. It is a simple step to begin this journey it is called 'release.' Release your mind to take God at God's word and believe that God has the power to do all things. Open yourself to be receptive to the move of God. Remember, when the exhausted and famished crowd that sat before Jesus listening to his word. The Disciples wanted to send them away because they did not have food to feed them. A little boy with five barley loaves and two small fish....Jesus took the loaves, gave thanks, and distributed to those who were seated... and he did the same with the fish....and fragments were taken...leftovers... Miracles. Anything that we place in the hands of Jesus, it can be resolved.

Wow! I am amazed at my journey...What a Ride. Who would believe that a daughter whose first home was a one room shack in the middle of a field, pulled cotton as a child whose first job paid $1.67 per hour would grow up to earn a Doctorate Degree from Southern Methodist University, Perkins School of Theology and travel the world? How did I stand on the Acropolis in Greece and Walk one of the 5 bridges of Prague? Why would I have been invited to do a Revival in Nassau, Bahamas or preach for the African Clergywomen's Consultation? I stood on the banks of the Euphrates in Africa and by the Baptismal Font of Lydia in Greece. I have laid my hands on the Pyramids of Egypt and walked the Via Dela Rosa in Jerusalem. My, my, my what awesome experiences for the woman of God who never held any high ranking positions, nor made the top salaries. How did it all take place? It is all by the grace of God, and when I look back over my life and consider what could have been, I am thankful. I am just an ordinary child of God who believes that nothing is impossible with God.

It has been my life's mission to touch the lives of the people that I encounter daily. Not every person receives, nor accepts your touch. There are so many people whose paths I have crossed. With some I spent many years, walking alongside of them sharing long talks and many emotions. With others, it was a brief moment in time. Many disappointed me, because I thought that we were doing the work of the Kingdom, but there were other agendas. Still others seemed happy to run ahead and throw rolling tackles to insure that my path was blocked, and opportunities were prohibited. And I recall with great joy those who walked beside me along this road called life. They consistently showed me their love and support and what a time we enjoyed. It took all of this to help me realize that not one of the naysayers have the power to prevent what God is going to do.

This is my story, and though I bring the journey of Ministry as a Pastor, leader, teacher to an end, my life continues. "Life is a mystery to be lived," as quoted by Adriana Trigiani. I have fully lived 71 years through the many vicissitudes of life. Death too is a mystery, one that we do not fully comprehend. We know that life come to cessation as we know it and none of our loved ones have come back to speak with us. We trust the holy writ which teaches us that by faith we receive the gift of eternal life,

Death has seemingly been a present reality with me. The death of my daddy, Jimmie Isaac, my nephew, Elnoris Isaac, Jr and my precious son, John C. Lee, III, all of these tragically. The death of my mother Mrs. Pearlie B. Isaac who fought a great battle in life. And the death of my husband, devoted John C. Lee, Jr. a faithful, devoted Christian, father, grandfather and family man. And there is there is the death of our 'babysister' Evangelist Sheila Isaac, whom I loved and deeply miss. She was my intercessory Prayer Warrior, confidant and midnight conversationalist. Gone far too soon for me.

As I sit alone at night, or when I need emergency medical attention I miss all of them. However, I am confident in the faith of our Lord and Savior Jesus Christ that they are with our God. Many conversation were shared with my sister about how long we planned to live. My plan is to live to be 100 and she would say, "Why do you want to life that long?" We discussed health care issues, heart conditions and I would share, "I work out because I want to strengthen my heart."

Life, no matter how long one prepares comes to an end on its own terms. But I believe, and have taught others that on the 'other-side' in 'our heavenly place' there is a home prepared for us. A good God who has allowed us to live through such difficult situations in life is going to welcome us home someday. Until then, my journey continues through faith believing that there are many I will meet on the other side.

In the words of the Old Hymn. "Sing the wondrous love of Jesus. Sing His mercy and his grace. In the mansions bright and blessed, He's prepared for us a place. When we all get to heaven what a day of rejoicing that will be. When we all see Jesus We'll sing and shout the victory." Until then, I will continue to give God all of the praise and the glory for the awesome journey that I have lived thus far. Wow What A Ride!!!

EPILOGUE

God loves you and wants to give you the desire of your heart!

I am not an unusual person, an ordinary country girl with big dreams of traveling the world. Everyone has different dreams, and I would recommend that you anchor your life in our Lord and Savior Jesus Christ. Give your best in service and you will find that the best will come back to you.

Several years ago, there was a gospel song entitled Touch Somebody's Life, and these are some of the words that I remember:

Touch somebody's life with your goodness

Touch somebody's life with a helping hand,

Touch somebody's life with understanding,

You'll be surprise how soon that same touch comes back to you.

It is my prayer that the story of my life will inspire and encourage you. It is the story of a young person whose life was touched in so many ways by people whose examples made a difference for me. At an early age, I learned the word faith, and the biblical meaning and have tried to exercise it all along my journey. I learned that forgiven sins no longer had control over my life. I learned that God has unconditional love for everyone, meaning for me that even when I felt unloved God loved me. I learned that failure is not in the falling, it is in the staying down. And I learned to turn each stumbling block into a stepping stone. Oh yes, and that it is impossible to hold someone else down and move forward at the same time. And unless you are willing to forgive, you cannot be forgiven.

Life has been an adventure, and a journey. Release yourself and give yourself to Jesus and you will be surprised what God has in store for you. Learn from my lessons that defeat only comes when you are willing to give up. But if you put your whole trust in God you will face challenges in your life, but you can be assured that God will empower you to get through the journey. There are times that you may have to wait. And know this, "And we know that all things work together for those that love the Lord and are called according to his purpose," Romans 8:28.

Every life ends in a whisper. "Why, you do not even know what will happen tomorrow. What is your life? You are a mist that appears for a little while and then vanishes," James 4:14 (NIV). I am so thankful for the journey and truly it has been a ride. What I invite each reader to do is to live your life to the full and know that God has a purpose for each of our lives. If God has called you for a specific purpose that may not make you feel very comfortable, step forward anyway and know that you never know the life that you may touch to make a real difference.